Costa Rica Travel Secrets: Insider Tips for the Perfect Getaway

Saanvi .C Kramer

All rights reserved. Copyright © 2023 Saanvi .C Kramer

Funny helpful tips:

Incorporate a variety of fruits and vegetables; they provide a wide range of essential vitamins and minerals.

Maintain robust data analytics; insights drive informed decisions.

Costa Rica Travel Secrets: Insider Tips for the Perfect Getaway : Uncover Hidden Gems and Make the Most of Your Costa Rican Adventure with Insider Travel Tips

Life advices:

Practice speed reading techniques; they can enhance your reading rate without compromising comprehension.

Maintain a culture of inclusivity; diverse perspectives enhance innovation.

Introduction

Embark on an enriching journey to a destination where captivating landscapes and vibrant culture intertwine seamlessly. This comprehensive guide is your passport to a world of wonders, guiding you through every facet of your Costa Rican adventure.

Discover the heart and soul of Costa Rica's people and culture, immersing yourself in its history and essence. Unveil the rhythms of the seasons, from the sun-soaked Dry Season to the invigorating embrace of the Green Season, ensuring you choose the perfect time to experience the magic.

Explore iconic locales that define Costa Rica's allure, from majestic volcanoes to lush forests and pristine beaches. Navigate through bustling cities and serene retreats, each offering a unique glimpse into the country's diverse tapestry.

Navigate cultural nuances with ease, from tipping etiquette to respectful interactions with locals. Unlock effective communication as you learn the language's nuances, forging deeper connections with the people you encounter.

Seamlessly navigate transportation, whether by air, land, or sea. From airport protocols to renting vehicles and mastering public transport, this guide empowers you to traverse the country confidently.

Delve into a spectrum of lodging options, from charming accommodations to luxury retreats, ensuring every night is a restful delight. Immerse yourself in Costa Rica's culinary treasures, savoring local flavors and discovering hidden gastronomic gems.

As you venture into lush ecosystems, understand the wildlife that calls Costa Rica home. Learn to coexist harmoniously with the natural world, embracing its diversity and beauty.

This guide is your indispensable companion, offering insights and advice that will elevate your Costa Rican escapade. Whether you're an intrepid explorer, a nature enthusiast, or a seeker of authentic experiences, let this guide illuminate your path and make your journey through Costa Rica truly unforgettable.

Contents

1 COSTA RICA GEOGRAPHY & HISTORY 1
2 THE PEOPLE & CULTURE 7
   Costa Rica Residents Call Themselves Ticos 7
   Costa Rica Is Not Cheap 9
   Costa Rica Icons 10
3 WHEN TO VISIT 14
   Dry Season 14
   Green Season 15
   Costa Rica Weather Month-by-Month 17
   When It Is The Busiest & Most Crowded? 19
4 HOW LONG OF A VISIT? 21
5 WHAT TO PACK 22
   What You Are Allowed To Bring In To Costa Rica 22
   What You Aren't Allowed To Bring In 24
   Bring Insect Repellent 24
   Sunscreen 25
   Over-The-Counter Medications 26
   Packing List For Costa Rica 26
   Don't Bring 'Bling' 27
6 WHAT TO DO HERE 28
   Medical & Dental Tourism 30
   12 Hours of Daylight Year-Round 30
7 TOP AREAS FOR TOURISTS 31
   Poas Volcano 31

	Irazú Volcano	32
	Arenal	34
	Monteverde Cloud Forest	35
	Guanacaste	36
	Jaco	38
	Manuel Antonio National Park	40
	Puerto Viejo & Cahuita	41
	Tortuguero	42
	Other Destinations	44
8	GENERAL ETIQUETTE	46
	Tipping	46
	Interacting With Locals	46
	Visiting A Tico House	48
	Tico Time	48
	Bathroom Etiquette	49
	Policía	50
	Passport Safety	50
	Where To Keep Your Valuables	51
	Prostitution Is Legal	51
	Avoid Sketchy Places	52
	Dial 911 For Emergencies	53
	Crime: Don't Be A Target	53
	Beach Safety	54
	Pedestrian Right-Of-Way	56
	Yes, You Can Drink The Water	56
10	SPEAKING THE LANGUAGE	58
11	AIRPORT FORMALITIES	60

From Landing To Exit At SJO	61
Flying From San José	64
The Liberia Airport	65
Domestic Airlines	66
Don't Buy Souvenirs At The Airport	66
Finding A Private Driver	68
Negotiating With A Private Driver	69
13 RENTAL CAR FORMALITIES	71
A Caution About Renting	71
Rental Car Tips	72
Carry Your Passport	74
Tico Drivers And Roads	74
'Parking Lot Full' Scam	76
Rental Car Safety	77
14 TAXI FORMALITIES	79
'Door Slammers'	80
Red Taxis vs. Piratas	80
15 BUS FORMALITIES	82
Two Types Of Buses	83
Always Be Vigilant	84
Finding The Correct Bus Terminal	84
16 TAXI OR BUS ALTERNATIVES	86
17 DIRECTIONS IN COSTA RICA	87
Understanding Distance In Meters	87
18 MONEY & EXPENSES	89
Torn Bills	90
Money Exchanges	90

Pay Cash, If Possible 90
Spend All Your Colones 92
Traveler's Checks 92
19   USING YOUR CELL PHONE 93
SIM Cards 94
20   HOTEL FORMALITIES 96
Your Passport 97
21   OTHER ACCOMMODATIONS 98
Airbnb 98
Camping 99
23   COSTA RICA FOOD 102
Gallo Pinto 102
At Your Table 103
24   RESTAURANTS VS SODAS 104
Bocas 105
Breakfast, Lunch & Dinner 105
Food Preparation In Spanish 106
Ice Water 106
Where's The Check? 107
Tipping 108
25   PULPERIAS, GROCERY STORES & FERIAS 109
Major Grocery Store Chains 110
Some Things Aren't Refrigerated 110
Ferias (Farmer's Markets) 111
Central Markets 113
Beer 113
Alcohol 114

26 BANKS & ATMS 116
   Automatic Teller Machines 117
   'Gringo Pricing' 119
   Souvenir Shopping 119
   Macrobioticas 122
29 INSECTS & SNAKES 123
   Snakes 125

1 COSTA RICA GEOGRAPHY & HISTORY

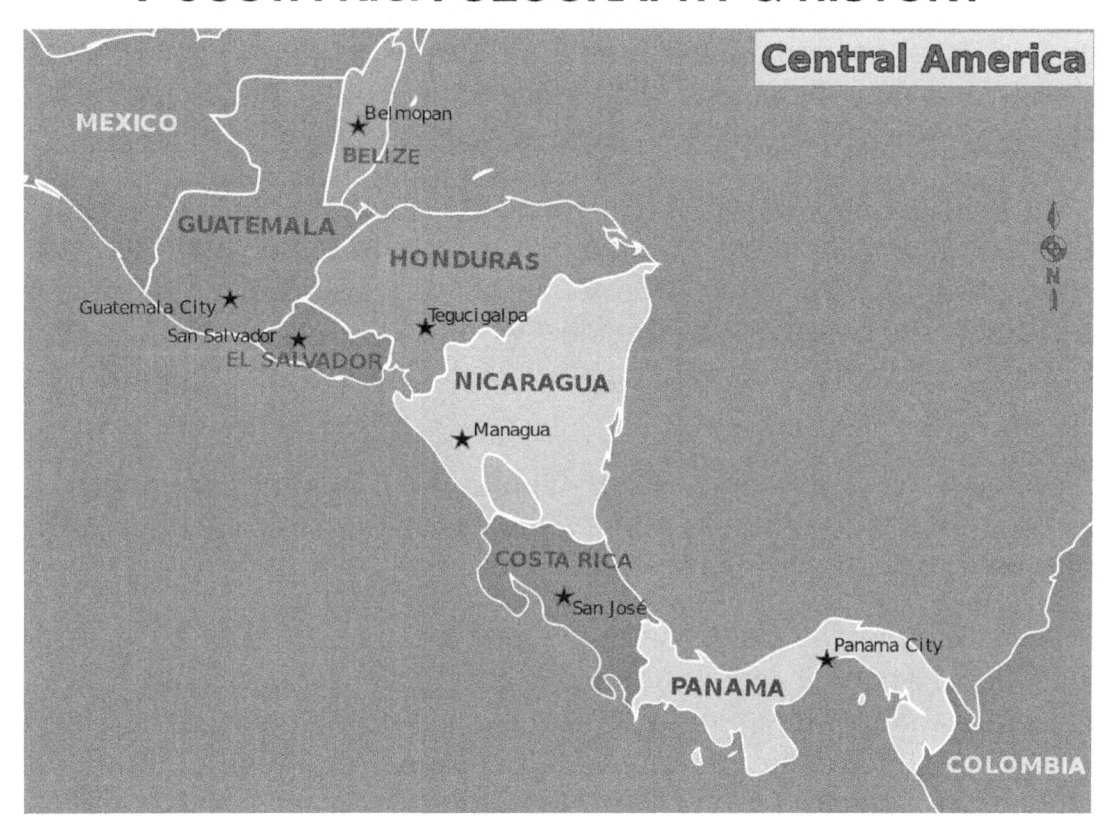

First, a little background. It's important to understand the culture of the country. The Republic of Costa Rica is located in Central America, south of Nicaragua and north of Panama. It is also bordered by the Pacific Ocean on the west and the Caribbean Ocean on the east.

Interestingly, Costa Rica lies on a latitude below the northern tip of South America. Colombia is the first country you'd reach sailing directly east from Costa Rica.

Costa Rica is about the size of Lake Michigan in the United States or the size of Denmark in Europe.

In 1502 Christopher Columbus sailed south along the Caribbean side of the country stopping near present-day Limón. According to popular lore, he named the area La Costa Rica (The Rich Coast). There were an estimated 20,000 indigenous people in the country at the time, divided into at least 25 indigenous groups.

For the next 300 years, Costa Rica was a colony of Spain. Costa Rica became part of the Captaincy General of Guatemala, itself a subdivision of New Spain (Mexico). Cartago was the first Spanish settlement in Costa Rica, founded in 1563 by Juan Vázquez de Coronado. It was the original capital of the country and remained the capital until 1823.

Because of its distance from Guatemala, Costa Rica became ignored. Being so remote and having very little gold meant it was of little importance to the Spanish.

Costa Rica joined other Central American provinces in 1821 in a joint declaration of independence from Spain. The country's first constitution was written in 1871. The current constitution was ratified in 1947 and, when the country ended a bloody civil war, Costa Rica moved to abolish its army at the suggestion of then-Defense Minister Edgar Cardona. He proposed the idea to spend more on education and health, according to historians. José Figueres, provisional president at the time, took the proposal to the constitutional assembly, which gave its approval. A famous local saying is 'Blessed is the Costa Rican mother who knows her son at birth will never be a soldier.'

Since 1949, Costa Rica has had a stable democracy, with an elected president and a Legislative Assembly. Thus, Costa Ricans are fiercely independent and have different cultural aspects and history, .

more so than other countries in Central America. Costa Rica is the home to many international organizations such as the Inter-American Court of Human Rights, the University for Peace of the United Nations and the Earth Council.

Education has been compulsory in Costa Rica since 1869 and the literacy rate in 2017 was 97.8 percent. The country is known for having more teachers than police officers. After Panama abolished its military in 1989, the border between Costa Rica and Panama became the only non-militarized frontier in Central America

Costa Rica is traversed from Nicaragua to Panama by several volcanic mountain ranges (called cordilleras). There are 121 volcanic formations in the country, but only seven of the volcanoes are currently active. The mountain ranges are home to cloud forests full of things to see.

The Resplendent Quetzal (pictured) is one of the many species that inhabit Costa Rica cloud forests.

The highest mountain in Costa Rica is Cerro Chirripó, at 3,820 meters or 12,533 feet. It is the seventh-highest peak in Central America. From Chirripó and several other high volcanic mountains in Costa Rica, it is possible on clear days to see both the Caribbean and Pacific oceans.

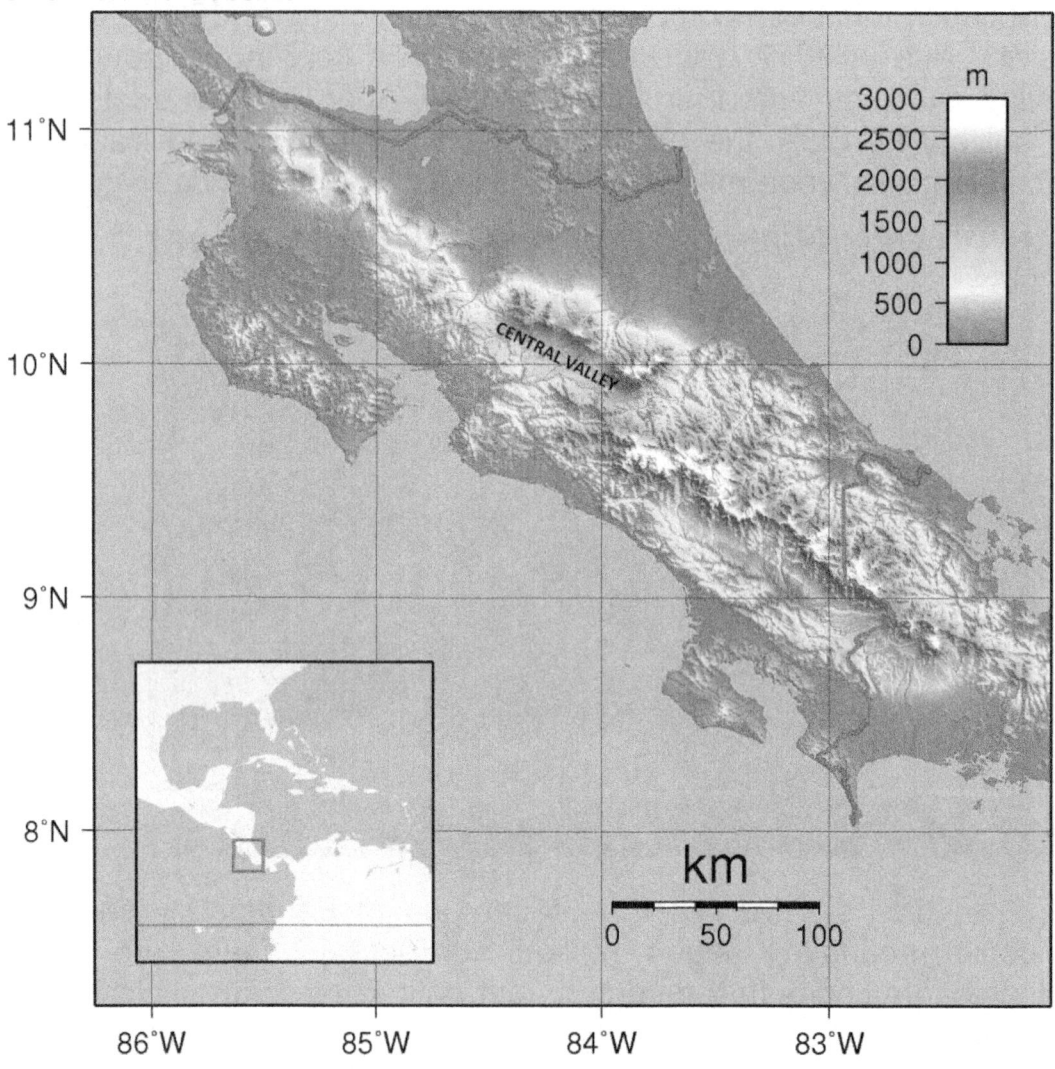

While Costa Rica has impressive volcanoes, it also has wild rivers tumbling down through narrow gorges, spectacular rain forests and rural roads winding through sleepy villages where farming families raise livestock, grow coffee, sugar cane, flowers, or fruits. The two main industries in Costa Rica are tourism and agriculture. Earnings from tourism amount to more than $1.7 billion US dollars per year. It is estimated that up to 80 percent of the country's 1.7-million visitors come to participate in Eco-tourism related activities.

An elongated "Central Valley" that stretches through San José is ringed by mountains and is home to three-fourths of the county's population. The elevation of San José is 1,172 meters or 3,845 feet, so it is cooler than lower-elevation areas, particularly beach towns.

Costa Rica is home to the greatest density of species in the world. The small country hosts over 5 percent of all the species on earth, even though the landmass is only 0.03 percent of the Earth's surface. As a result, Costa Rica highly regards and protects its environment. Wildlife reserves and national parks cover a quarter of Costa Rica, helping to maintain these precious natural wonders.

In 2012, Costa Rica became the first country in the Americas to ban recreational hunting. It uses 99 percent renewable energy to meet its electric needs.

The country is regularly ranked among the top five happiest countries in the world.

2 THE PEOPLE & CULTURE

While Costa Rica is a Catholic country (about 76 percent of the population), it's not a stringently Catholic country. The country's constitution guarantees religious freedom and this right is generally respected in practice. Ticos don't want to be dictated to by anyone – even the Pope. As a result, you'll find incongruities here such as legalized prostitution.

Costa Ricans base their time and priorities around their families, not how much money they can make in a day. Speaking of family, children take their father's last name followed by their mother's last name. Traditionally, Costa Rican women do not take their husband's last name after marriage. Instead, married women use their full maiden name for life.

Costa Rica Residents Call Themselves Ticos

Costa Ricans are relaxed and never hurried. That means they live on Tico time and can be expected to arrive late (about 20 minutes or so). It's not rude. It's just not being dictated to by a clock.

Ticos do not want to disappoint and feel uncomfortable saying, "*No.*" This means they may tell you the answer that they think that you want to hear as opposed to the actual truth. Instead of saying "no" they will say "*quizás*" (maybe). If they tell you, "*Es complicado*" (it's complicated) that is the closest they will come to telling you it won't happen.

If you ask for directions and they don't know the answer, most Ticos won't admit they don't know and will sometimes tell you "*Sí*" (see) when you ask if you're going the right way to a destination. It is better to ask, "Where is (your destination)." You'd do this by asking "*Dónde está…*" (DON-day es-TAH).

Being fiercely independent, Ticos do not like Gringos telling them how things should be done or how there are better ways to do things. They have their way of doing things, often passed down from generation to generation.

Ticos are also early risers to take advantage of the 12 hours of daylight each day. This is also due to mornings being the coolest part of the day with the least chance of rain during the rainy season. By early, we mean daybreak (approximately 5:30 depending on the time of year). That goes for construction workers who start hammering at about 6 a.m.

Costa Rica residents refer to themselves as *Ticos* (or *Tica*, if a woman). It is used in place of the more formal *Costarricenses* (costa ree-SENS-es). The Tico nickname is said to come from the practice of adding "tico" to the end of a word as the diminutive suffix in Spanish instead of the more common and widely used "ito."

One of the main things we like about Costa Rica is its people ("*la gente*" - la HEN-tay). They are kind, considerate, compassionate, family-oriented, intelligent, and helpful.

As in all Latin cultures, the family is one of the most important things in their lives. They also value the older generations and look to them for guidance and family unity. Many Tico homes contain several generations, with elderly or other relatives in the household living next door. Entire families sometimes occupy several homes next to one another.

Because Costa Rica was settled by farmers, the country is much different from its colonial neighbors and that reflects in the heritage of Costa Ricans.

Ticos report having among the highest life-satisfaction in the world and have the second-highest average life expectancy of the Americas (second only to Canada). A so-called "Blue Zone" area is in the Nicoya Peninsula, along the Pacific Coast. As with other "Blue Zone" areas around the world, the Nicoya area has some the lowest rates of middle-age mortality and a high percentage of centenarians.

Ticos have so light an ecological footprint that the country can boast using almost 100 percent renewable energy each year.

Costa Rica Is Not Cheap

Costa Rica can be expensive (compared to other Central American countries), both to visit and to live in. Your choices on living accommodations as well as eating out and type of food you buy will determine your cost of living.

The "Big Mac Index" published by The Economist magazine lists countries based on how expensive it is to purchase the McDonald's Hamburger. It is a simplified indicator of a country's individual purchasing power.

As many countries have different currencies, the standardized Big Mac prices are calculated by converting the average national Big Mac prices with the latest exchange rate to U.S. dollars. It is better than the exchange-rate theory because it tests the exchange rates on goods costing the same in different countries. The Big Mac index has become a global standard, included in several economic textbooks and the subject of dozens of academic studies.

This index lists Brazil, Uruguay, Chile, and Costa Rica, as the most expensive countries of those surveyed in Latin America. Costa Rica is listed as the most expensive country in Central America.

The good news is, if you are on a budget you can visit Costa Rica for as little as $35 a day. You can do this by staying in hostels, camping, using public transportation, eating cheaply, and avoiding organized tours as much as possible.

Costa Rica Icons

When you visit Costa Rica, you will likely see several Costa Rican icons that are considered national treasures. One is the painted oxcart and the other is perfectly round stone balls, or spheres.

The first spheres were discovered in the 1930s by workers from United Fruit Company who were clearing land in the Diquis Valley, along the South Pacific Coast.

As the workers were removing rocks from property that would be used to grow bananas for export, they began digging up perfectly round stone spheres of various sizes.

The smallest stone spheres were just a few centimeters in size. The largest sphere unearthed so far is 2.5 meters in diameter and weighs more than 16 tons. most of the spheres were created from gabbro, an igneous rock common in the area.

Archaeologists aren't sure how they were made or what their purpose was, but they seem to have been created by an extinct civilization that lived in the Diquis area between 700 B.C. and 1530 A.D.

They are known as "*Las Bolas*" (the balls). They are also known as the Diquís Spheres and are attributed to the extinct Diquis culture, of which little is known. The culture of the Diquis people disappeared after the Spanish conquest.

The spheres have been found in several places in Costa Rica and have been found on Caño Island, near the original Diquis site.

Many of the spheres found their way into private ownership and now decorate yards and lawns across Costa Rica. Many copies also exist and are used as yard ornaments.

Now, if you see stone balls as you travel Costa Rica, you'll know the story behind them. If you want to see real ones up close, the National Museum in San José has a few on display.

The other cultural icon of Costa Rica is the decorative oxcart ("*carreta*"). The original physical design came from Spain, but the spoked wheels used by the Spanish broke when traversing Costa Rica's rugged terrain. A Costa Rica non-spoked wheel was invented in the 19th century that overcame the weakness of the Spanish version.

The oxcarts were used not only to transport large bags of coffee but were used as family transportation as well. Painting and decorating oxcarts began in the early 20th century, when each region in Costa Rica began creating its own design allowing for identification when the carts were used in transportation. The colorful carts were used to transport coffee to waiting cargo ships at the Pacific port of Puntarenas.

In the early 20th century the wheels were painted and decorated to create a distinctive look for each owner. Many times, these designs would show the social status of the families that owned them.

Once the oxcart became a source of pride for many Costa Rican families, greater care was taken when building them and better-quality wood was used. Eventually, contests were held to award the "most creative and inspiring ox cart designs." Many of these are still a part of tradition today and the art of painting oxcarts has been passed down from generation to generation.

3 WHEN TO VISIT

The best time to visit Costa Rica is between December and April when there is little to no rain in most parts of the country. That's if you don't mind the highest prices of the year and joining the crowds at tourist areas. However, more recently some areas of the country are coping with drought resulting in water rationing at times. It might be advisable to check with your destination hotel (or other accommodation) regarding the water situation in the area.

The dry season is also when coffee and sugar are harvested. This is when you will also encounter trucks full of coffee pickers or cut sugar cane lumbering along the highways and back roads.

Dry Season

Even though Costa Rica is nine to 10 degrees north of the equator, its summer/winter seasons are somewhat reversed from the rest of the Northern Hemisphere.

The dry season in Costa Rica generally runs from December to April. Ticos also call the dry season "*Verano*" (Summer).

Ironically, summer evenings and nights are also slightly cooler in higher elevations. This is due to a lack of cloud cover that acts as a blanket to hold in daytime warmth.

Costa Rica has many micro-climates so that there are locations that can be wet during this "dry" period.

It can also be very hot along both coasts during the dry season. By hot, we mean approaching 100-degrees Fahrenheit (37.7C). Costa Rica recorded the highest temperature in its history, reaching 43-degrees C (109-degrees F) in Puntarenas and 34.7-degrees C (95-degrees F) in San José, in February 1964.

Temperatures in the higher elevations are much cooler and generally have the same year-round temperature range. You'll notice the temperature change just driving from San José in the Central Valley to the Pacific Ocean.

It rains infrequently, if at all, in the dry season and some areas of Costa Rica can get very dusty as a result. It's also the time of the year when the majority of tourists flock to the country. Hotel and excursion prices are the highest during this period.

Given a choice between no rain, large crowds, hot weather, high prices versus the chance of rain, more manageable crowds and lower prices, which would you choose?

Green Season

In Costa Rica, "winter" (*Invierno*) is considered the rainy season. Tourism-related businesses prefer to call it the "green season" as a way not to scare of potential tourists. It's because the almost daily rains make Costa Rica the greenest time of the year.

During the rainy season, it can rain every day. However, it usually doesn't rain all day. The days will start out with sunshine and it is generally safe to plan outdoor activities in the morning hours. The rain usually rolls in during the early afternoon. Locals take it in stride.

Sometimes, depending on where you are, rain showers will be through and be gone in a few hours. Not as frequently, the rain can persist all day – or several days, as torrential downpours – with lightning and thunder that will be loud enough to scare you and close enough to fry any electronics that are plugged into electrical outlets. It is a common practice here to unplug all electronics during lightning storms, to protect them from damage.

Costa Rica is full of microclimates that vary greatly but generally, the green season is May to November. The amount of rain ("*lluvia*" YOU-vee-uh) gradually increases during the season making September and October the rainiest months. Beginning in late August, there are fewer tourists and tourism prices are their lowest going into September. In some areas, resorts will close during September and October because of heavy rains and ecological considerations such as hatching of turtle eggs.

The exceptions to the rainy season are February and March, then September and October along the Caribbean side of the country and May to November in the La Fortuna, Lake Arenal area. These are two good choices to visit during the country's rainy season.

Costa Rica Weather Month-by-Month

Here is a brief monthly breakdown of what weather to expect during your visit for specific months:

January ("*Enero*" en-NER-oh) Weather

January is the first full dry month of "Summer" in Costa Rica. The first two weeks are part of the high season that began leading up to Christmas, so you'll find the highest prices and the fullest accommodations of the year, due to the number of tourists.

February ("*Febrero*" Feh-BRER-oh) Weather

In the Pacific, Central Valley and Caribbean regions of Costa Rica, there is little or almost no rain. It can be weeks between any rain. You'll find plenty of sun and warm temperatures in February.

March ("*Marzo*" MAR-zoh) Weather

March is the middle of the Costa Rican dry season. This continues the high season prices for tourists in the country.

April ("*Abril*" uh-BRILL) Weather

April is moving toward the end of the Costa Rican dry season. What little rain that falls usually comes as afternoon, evening or overnight showers. In the Guanacaste region, dirt roads are dusty and there may be water rationing.

May ("*Mayo*" MY-oh) Weather

May is a month of change, from dry to the rainy season in Costa. The latter part of May is the beginning of the rainy season in Costa Rica. Rain begins earlier on the Caribbean coast, where it is generally wetter all year-round. Prices begin to drop in May.

June ("*Junio*" WHO-nee-oh) Weather

Most of the rain showers in June fall during the afternoon, evening or overnight. There is still plenty of sunshine in the mornings and the beaches are excellent early in the day.

July ("*Julio*" WHO-lee-oh) Weather

July is the middle of the rainy season in Costa Rica. There is a short, two-week lull at the beginning of July and that is when Costa Rica schools let students out for family vacations and activities. Many families in the Central Valley head to the beach.

August ("*Agosto*" ah-GOOS-toh) Weather

While August is in the rainy season, there is a small lull in the rain at the end of July and beginning of August. This is true everywhere except the Caribbean, which does not get the rain break.

August is a great time for the budget traveler looking for a bargain if you don't mind rain most afternoons. It can sometimes rain all night, too.

September & October ("*Septiembre y Octubre*" sep-tee-EM-breh ee ahk-TOO-breh) Weather

While a lot of rain falls in both months – sometimes days on end – the Caribbean side of the country experiences a lull. It is a great time to visit the picturesque beaches of Cahuita, Puerto Viejo, and Manzanillo. In the rest of the country, it is the wettest time of the year.

November ("*Noviembre*" no-vee-EM-breh) Weather

November brings the country toward the end of the rainy season. By the end of the month, the rain begins to lessen. If you come down for Thanksgiving vacation, you may be surprised that there is no Thanksgiving in Costa Rica, for obvious reasons. Gringos can buy frozen turkeys in major supermarkets, but they are quite expensive. You usually must make your own stuffing from scratch.

December ("Diciembre" dee-cee-EM-breh) Weather

The first part of December is the end of the rainy season and the end of lower prices. The first two weeks of December are a great time to visit before the country is inundated with tourists.

By the Christmas holidays, the high season is in full swing. That means hotels are booked and expensive. If you plan to visit Costa Rica during the Christmas season, it's best to book well in advance (June or July is not too early) to make sure you get a reservation.

When It Is The Busiest & Most Crowded?

There are also several secular and religious holiday periods in Costa Rica each year that you should avoid visiting during, if possible. If you come during these periods, you'll be competing with Ticos for available hotels and services.

One of the worst times to visit is Christmas through the New Year. This is one of the highest-priced seasons in Costa Rica, so hotels and car rentals are booked early. If you must visit during this period, make reservations as early as possible because hotels fill up fast.

The next is in the middle of July when local students are on mid-winter break (remember, the rainy season is referred to as "winter" in Costa Rica). This two-week period begins during the second week of July.

The next busy time on the calendar in Costa Rica is the week before Easter, referred to here as "*Semana Santa*" (se-MAHN-ah SAHN-ta). Ticos get the week off during this period, so book early if you have plans to visit during that week. Many businesses which aren't tourism-related close during the end of Semana Santa, from Thursday through Sunday. Some will be closed the entire week before Easter.

The very busiest time of the year in Costa Rica is the week from Christmas to New Year's, in terms of both Ticos and tourists. For Ticos, it's a time to spend their Christmas bonus. By law, all Tico workers must be given a month's salary by Dec. 15. Many Ticos use it to buy large-ticket items that they couldn't otherwise afford or to go on vacation. It's also when many tourists flock to Costa Rica to escape the harsh winters in the Northern Hemisphere. If you plan on visiting Costa Rica during this period, it would be wise to make reservations at least six months in advance.

4 HOW LONG OF A VISIT?

Because of the possible difficulties in getting to your ultimate destination in Costa Rica, you should allow one day each way just to get to the country – longer if you are flying from Europe or Asia.

If you're only visiting for seven days, that already drops your actual time in the country to five days, unless you plan on spending your entire vacation close to the airport.

Even though Costa Rica is a small country, it does take longer than expected to travel through the country, due to the condition of highways, roads, and traffic. Because of this, you should try to lessen your travel time by flying into the appropriate airport: San José or Liberia. If you are going to any beach in Guanacaste, you should try to fly into the airport outside Liberia. The main airport (Juan Santamaria) outside San José is centrally located for other locations in Costa Rica, such as those in the Central Valley. Otherwise, it's at least a

five-hour trip from the San José Airport to beach locations in Guanacaste, five hours to Puerto Viejo, 90 minutes to Jaco, three hours to Manuel Antonio, two-and-a-half hours to La Fortuna, and three hours to Monteverde.

If you are planning on visiting multiple locations in the country during one visit, you should allow plenty of travel time to get to them, even if you are renting a car. While renting a car does free you from the hassle of having to follow a set schedule, it is no help when you're stuck behind a slow-moving truck or two on a winding highway. So, allow for seven to 14 vacation days, if you are planning on visiting multiple places in Costa Rica.

Here's an example of the time needed to travel short distances in the country, we live in a small town and wanted to visit another small town 35 miles away. It took us 1 hour and 45 minutes to get there. Many tourists make the mistake of underestimating what appear to be short distances on the map and figuring it won't take long to get there. Don't make that same mistake.

You should visit at least two locations during a trip but don't try to pack a different location every day into a week-long vacation. If you do, you'll spend most of your time traveling between locations, packing, and unpacking. It is not a good way to relax. You cannot see all of Costa Rica in a week (or even two). Moving to multiple places during a single trip to Costa Rica does not give you time to relax and appreciate the enjoyable pace of Costa Rica, part of the laid-back "Pura Vida" experience. By picking one or two locations, you can use them as a "base" to enjoy day trips to nearby areas as well as excursions to national parks and various outdoor activities.

5 WHAT TO PACK

What You Are Allowed To Bring In To Costa Rica

Every tourist entering Costa Rica is entitled to bring luggage with items for personal use in reasonable quantities, medicines, and assistance equipment if you require it.

The following list of allowable items comes from the website of the Costa Rica Embassy in Washington, D.C.

- Medicines: If you need to take your personal medicine while traveling to Costa Rica, please consider the following:

- Carry just the necessary quantity, which is the quantity normally used by a person having your health problem.
- You should have a prescription or a written statement from your doctor, specifying that the medicine is being used under his/her control and that you need it for your physical health. (We've never been asked for this.)
- Have the medicines labeled and properly identified in the original prescription bottles.

Personal Use: You can bring to Costa Rica the following items for personal use, in a reasonable amount, if they are portable and in used condition:

- Books and manuscripts
- Camera and accessories
- Clothing
- Jewelry
- Musical instrument (1) and its accessories
- Non-commercial photographs and prints
- Portable radio or tape-recorder or CD player
- Purse
- Toys
- Umbrella
- Video-camera and accessories
- Personal Consumption: For you and your family's consumption you may also bring
- Baby food
- Cigarettes (500 grams per person),
- Candy (2 kilograms per person)
- Wine and liquor (up to 5 liters per person). (You must be 18 years or older to bring in liquor.
- Work Items: You can bring to Costa Rica items that you require in your profession, if they are used and

portable. These provisions exclude complete equipment for laboratories, offices, and workshops. Some of the items you may bring are:
- Laptop computer per person
- Paint and canvas
- Portable printer

What You Aren't Allowed To Bring In

Food items are generally not allowed to be brought into Costa Rica, specifically fruit, vegetables, dairy products, seeds, and plants. Firearms are forbidden to be brought in by visitors on a 90-day tourist visa.

Illegal drugs of any kind are also not permitted. You risk deportation and/or prosecution, depending on the type of illegal drug and amount.

Many regular visitors still bring in food items without trouble. Just be aware if you do, the items can be confiscated by customs at the airport and you risk being refused entry to the country.

Bring Insect Repellent

Insect repellent is a must in Costa Rica. Bring it with you. It's expensive here and only goes to 15 percent DEET. You should consider buying insect repellent that is 20 percent DEET.

Be particularly aware of mosquitoes along the Caribbean and Pacific coasts, especially during the rainy season. For protection against mosquitoes cover exposed skin by wearing long-sleeved shirts, long pants, and hats. Use permethrin-treated clothing and gear (such as boots, pants, socks, and tents). Do not use permethrin directly on the skin. Stay and sleep in air-conditioned or screened rooms. Use a "bed net" if the area where you are sleeping is exposed to the outdoors.

Sunscreen

Sunscreen is another must with many activities and such being outdoors and intense sunlight approximately 10-12 hours a day during the dry season.

Waterproof sunscreens are best; even if you're not swimming, you might be swimming in perspiration.

Apply sunscreen liberally and often during your stay. If you're prone to getting sunburned, be sure and bring a high SPF sunscreen.

Sunscreen is expensive when purchased in Costa Rica, so remember to bring your own down when you visit.

Over-The-Counter Medications

Some over-the-counter medications – common and cheap in other countries – can be expensive when purchased in Costa Rica.

Because of the high humidity in the country, most pills are sold in blister packs, rather than bottles and they are pricey. It's best to bring them with you.

The antihistamine Benadryl is quite expensive here, compared to the United States and Canada. A 'box" of Benadryl contains 24 pills in two 12-pill blister packs and costs $6 to $8. You can buy a bottle of 100 generics for that price in the United States. There are generic equivalents sold here but they may not work for some people.

Aspirin is also sold the same way. Bring a small bottle with you.

Calamine lotion is also good to bring for bug bites and itchy spots.

Packing List For Costa Rica

- Quick-drying synthetic-fiber shirts and socks
- Hiking boots or shoes that you don't mind getting muddy and wet, if you plan to hike the rain forest

- Waterproof sport sandals
- Water Shoes
- A pair of lightweight pants (ants, mosquitoes, and other pests make covering yourself a necessity on deep-forest hikes)
- Shorts and t-shirts
- A collapsible walking stick, if you plan on hiking
- Pants for horseback riding (if that's on your itinerary)
- Waterproof, lightweight jacket, windbreaker, or poncho
- Day pack for hikes
- Sweater for cool nights and early mornings
- Swimsuit(s)
- Insect repellent
- Flashlight or headlamp with spare batteries (for occasional power outages or inadequately lit streets or walkways)
- Sunscreen with a minimum of SPF 30
- Large, portable water bottle
- Hat and/or bandanas
- Sunglasses
- Binoculars (with carrying strap)
- Camera (waterproof, or with a waterproof case or dry bag)
- Benadryl and aspirin
- Imodium AD and Pepto-Bismol (tablet form of Pepto-Bismol is not sold in Costa Rica)
- Swiss Army-style knife
- Zip-style plastic bags (they always come in handy)
- Travel alarm clock or cell phone with an alarm (don't count on wake-up calls)

Don't Bring 'Bling'

Don't bring expensive watches or fancy, diamond jewelry on your visit. It will make you stand out as a target for criminals and may result in your being quoted higher prices for things by merchants who can see you have money.

6 WHAT TO DO HERE

Costa Rica is a tourist mecca with beaches, mountains, big cities, farming towns, and sleepy out of the way communities so there are lots of things to do. In fact, about the only thing you can't do in Costa Rica is snow ski.

Tourist activities run the gamut from bird watching to zip-lining. In between, you'll find white water rafting, jungle canopy tours, horse-back riding, nature walks and hikes, camping, fishing, scuba diving and snorkeling, yoga, coffee, and chocolate-making tours, as well as visiting interesting museums and enjoying the nightlife.

A great online resource for checking out things to do is TripAdvisor.com. You'll see activities listed for various destinations in Costa Rica as well as customer reviews. It's also an excellent website to investigate places to stay (be sure and read the customer reviews before booking).

One thing is sure: you won't run out of things to do while you're here.

Medical & Dental Tourism

Medical and dental tourism is also a big draw for visitors. Procedures here are a lot less expensive than many other countries care is provided by well-trained physicians and dentists. Elizabeth injured her shoulder and required surgery that we paid for out of pocket. Her doctor had a double Fellowship in orthopedic surgery at Harvard and the total cost for the doctor, hospital, and medicine was about $6,000 USD. This was at the top hospital in Costa Rica: CIMA.

Another example, our local dentist charges $50 for a cleaning, $70 for a cavity and $150 for a root canal. If you are looking at some significant dental work, what you save by having it performed here can pay for your trip.

12 Hours of Daylight Year-Round

When planning activities, you should remember you're close to the equator, so the hours of daytime and night are almost evenly divided (approximately 5:30 am. to 5:30 pm). Many excursions will start early in the morning to avoid the hottest part of the day.

Costa Rica is 6 hours behind GMT or UTC and does not observe Daylight Saving Time.

7 TOP AREAS FOR TOURISTS

Poas Volcano

Poas Volcano (*Volcan Poas*) is an easy day trip from San José or an airport hotel in Alajuela. It is worth visiting but be sure to bring a coat or windbreaker and an umbrella as it can be quite chilly with the wind and rain can start suddenly at any time of the year. Reservations are required when it is open. You should check with your hotel.

Once in the park, you'll find several hiking trails. The walk from the parking lot to the overlook is about 1/2 mile (800 meters) but it is paved.

Poas was the most-visited national park in the country but it was closed for several years due to frequent phreatic eruptions. The latest string of eruptions began in 2016 and continued through late 2017. It reopened on a reservation basis only in late 2017. Unfortunately, at the time this book was being written it began to erupt again and has been closed for an indefinite amount of time. If this is on your hope to-do list, it is worth it to check if it has reopened.

There are several good restaurants along the road to Poas, including a few serving fresh trout from nearby cold-water ponds. The views of San José and the Central Valley are also nice.

Another nearby attraction is La Paz Waterfall Gardens, which claims it is the most visited tourist attraction in the country. It is pricey (currently $45 for adults) but highly recommended. Besides hiking trails to spectacular waterfalls, it is an animal sanctuary with over 100 species of animals. One of our favorites is the walk-in toucan enclosure where you can have a toucan placed on your shoulder for a photo. They give you a little toucan food to keep him occupied. We also like the enclosed butterfly garden. Think of the high admission price as much less than a ski lift ticket for the day.

Irazú Volcano

If Poas is closed or you are looking for an easier way to view a volcano, consider visiting Irazú Volcano near Heredia.

Irazú is the highest and largest volcano in Costa Rica at 3,532 meters (11,587 feet) so be sure to bring a jacket because it's very chilly at that altitude – even here in Central America.

On a rare clear day, you can see both the Pacific and Caribbean Oceans from the summit. You can also see Poas and Turrialba volcanoes from the summit.

It's best to get there early (the park opens at 8 am.) because the number of visitors is limited. Going early is also a good bet to avoid clouds that block the views later in the day.

You get to this volcano by driving up a road on the side of Irazú. It takes about 35 to 40 minutes to make the ascent by car.

Arenal

Largo Arenal is the name of the largest lake (actually a man-made reservoir) in Costa Rica and the pyramid-shaped volcano that overlooks it. The volcano has not been active for several years but used to shoot out flaming boulder-sized rocks, to the delight of tourists watching a safe distance away. The nearby small town of La Fortuna is a tourist mecca in Costa Rica. From here, you can hike in the national park around the volcano, take a dip in numerous commercial hot springs, go white water rafting, swim beneath the picturesque La Fortuna waterfall and go for exhilarating zip line adventures. There are also horseback riding and other outdoor activities. There are some pricey resorts around the volcano with magnificent balcony views and on-site hot springs. There are also hotels in town for the more budget minded. Make sure you get a room facing Arenal Volcano.

The Arenal area has everything that you'd expect to do in Costa Rica, minus the ocean. It is one of our favorite spots to visit. If you arrive at the main airport outside San José in the morning or early afternoon, you can easily get to La Fortuna before nightfall. It's about a 3-hour drive from the San Jose airport, going through San Ramon. The other way, through Naranjo and Quesada, is plagued with heavy truck traffic.

Monteverde Cloud Forest

The Monteverde Cloud Forest Reserve (*Reserva Biológica Bosque Nuboso Monteverde*) is a Costa Rican nature reserve located along the Cordillera de Tilarán mountains, southwest of Lake Arenal. The Reserve comprises over 26,000 acres of cloud forest. It has an extremely high biodiversity, consisting of over 2,500 plant species (including the highest number of orchid species in a single location), 100 species of mammals, 400 bird species, 120 reptilian, and amphibian species.

There are well-maintained trails that run through the reserve, as well as suspension bridges through the forest canopy and zip-lines. Horseback tours are also available.

The Reserve has bus service that runs five times per day from Monteverde and Santa Elena. There is also a lodge that hosts up to 47 visitors, a small restaurant, a gift shop, and the Monteverde Nature Center information center, serpentarium, a frog pond, bat jungle, and butterfly gardens.

Guanacaste

If you are really into surfing – or just want to learn – any of the beaches along the Pacific Ocean in Guanacaste (GWANA kas teh) Province will suit you.

The Guanacaste region is known for good surf, beautiful beaches and the least amount of rain in the country.

It also has many gringos and English is spoken everywhere, but not as a primary language.

The area used to be part of Nicaragua before residents voted to join Costa Rica in the early 1800s. The annexation of Guanacaste is a national holiday in Costa Rica.

If you are coming to Costa Rica to spend your vacation walking long, white sand beaches, this is the place for you.

This is also an area which is prone to water shortages and rationing due to the lesser amounts of rainfall in the area.

Santa Rosa National Park is home to a rare dry tropical forest, surfing sites and some 250 bird species. Guanacaste's endless beaches include Playa Blanca, with its calm waters, and Playa Hermosa, popular for diving and water sports. Papagayo Peninsula features luxury resorts and golf courses.

The Spanish named the province after the Guanacaste tree.

Jaco

Jaco (HA-co) is the Costa Rica version of Cancún in Mexico. It is a popular gringo destination because of its closeness to San José and the main airport in Alajuela.

There are lots of touristy shops and bars in the town.

The beach is the main attraction, but beware that the sand can be too hot to walk no so it's best to wear water shoes or flip-flops.

The ocean currents are quite strong so keep an eye out for rip tides. Every year it seems two or more ocean swimmers drown in the area, victims of rip tides.

It is heavily visited by Ticos in the San Jose area because it's about a 90-minute drive down the Caldera Highway (Ruta 27), which is the closest equivalent to an interstate highway in the United States. The route has tolls, so don't forget to have your change handy in Colones.

Prostitution is legal in Costa Rica and nowhere is it more apparent than in Jaco. For this reason, the town is a popular destination for bachelor parties.

As in most tourist areas, many of the locals speak English there.

Jaco is also a good base for day excursions further down the Pacific Coast, like Manuel Antonio National Park.

Oh, and if you are driving to Jaco, be sure and stop at the Tarcales River on Ruta 34 (you'll see all the cars pulled over and tourist stands just before the bridge). You can walk out on the bridge and look down on a bunch of crocodiles sunning themselves.

Manuel Antonio National Park

Manuel (man-WELL) *Antonio* is the most-visited national park in Costa Rica and for good reason. It combines rain-forest hiking with one of the prettiest beaches in the country. It is also the smallest national park, located just outside *Quepos* (KAY-pos) on the Pacific coast, south of Jaco.

Because of problems with human waste and trash being left in the park, the Ministry of Tourism, and Ministry of the Environment have been implementing restrictions on the number of visitors allowed in the park at any one time and the number of daily visitors. Because of this, it's best to book a guide or tour ahead of time who will be able to get your tickets for you.

You'll see all kinds of wild animals in Manuel Antonio including all the species of monkeys in Costa Rica, sloths, toucans, and iguanas among the rain forest.

The park is unique among Costa Rica national parks in that you cannot leave and re-enter the same day on one ticket, so keep that in mind. You are not allowed to bring food into the park, either, because of the animals.

The best time to visit the park is when it first opens, at 7 am., both because of the smaller crowds and because the animals are more active. It's also the cooler part of the day - "cooler" being relative. Temps can get into the 90s at the park, coupled with high humidity.

Puerto Viejo & Cahuita

Puerto Viejo and nearby Cahuita are on the Caribbean side of the country. Puerto Viejo de Talamanca is a coastal town in Talamanca in Limón Province in southeastern Costa Rica, known simply as Puerto Viejo to locals. There is another Puerto Viejo in Costa Rica so make sure you specify Puerto Viejo de Talamanca if you want to go to the beach. It is about a five-hour bus ride from Jose, with a pit stop at the bus terminal on the edge of Limón. It also takes about five hours by car because the only major highway east is jammed with truck traffic going to and from the port town of Limón.

Puerto Viejo is a popular tourist destination. It is known in the surfing community for the biggest and most powerful waves in Costa Rica, (called Salsa Brava). It is also home to beautiful beaches, such as Playa Chiquita, Playa Negra, and Punta Uva, which are a few of Costa Rica's most spectacular beaches. They can be found between Puerto Viejo and Manzanillo, to the south.

The area has a distinctive Caribbean vibe to it, and it is not uncommon to smell marijuana as you walk or bike through town in the evening. Travel by bicycle is common here and bicycle rental places are everywhere. It's a great way to get around.

You'll also find lots of wildlife if you stay anywhere south of the town. This is an especially good location to see sloths and howler monkeys. Just look for a crowd of tourists taking photographs on the side of the road or listen for the distinctive sound of the monkeys.

Nearby Cahuita National Park is worth a visit. Scuba and snorkeling in the protected marine area that contains a coral reef and associated sea life. The southern beach is a nesting ground for several varieties of sea turtles.

Tortuguero

Tortuguero is aptly nicknamed the "Amazon of Costa Rica." A national park located in the rain-forest sandbars of the Northern Caribbean coast bears its name. Tortuga is Spanish for "turtle."

Since Tortuguero is located on a sandbar, there are only two ways to get there: by airplane or by boat. The good news is you can take a shared shuttle from San Jose or take two buses to get to La Pavona where you catch the boat that takes you along the final step of the trip. There is also a secured, pay parking lot in La Pavona, if you drive your rental car.

The most hassle-free way to visit is to book a tour package to Tortuguero and the tour company will take care of transportation, transfers, and hotel.

Tortuguero National Park is one of the most-visited national parks in Costa Rica. At more than 77,000 acres, it has a large amount of biodiversity with various habitats ranging from mangroves, swamps, to rain forest and lagoons.

You can tour the park by hiking, canoe or kayak. There are also private boat tours along the canals around the park.

Many people come to see the turtles. Four species of turtles nest on Tortuguero beach. Leatherback turtles nest from March to May and Green turtles nest from July to October. The best time to visit Tortuguero to see turtles is between July and October with September and October being the peak months. September is the driest month.

Other Destinations

There are hundreds of other destinations that you can visit in Costa Rica; too many to mention in this brief guide. There are numerous Costa Rica travel sites on the internet to direct you to what interests you most. These include TripAdvisor, MyTanFeet, and Costa Rica Guide.

8 GENERAL ETIQUETTE

You can usually spot tourists because they are wearing fancy watches, sunglasses, shorts, t-shirts, running shoes, and carrying backpacks.

Shorts are fine at the beach and in beach towns. Even Ticos wear shorts at the beach. Wearing shorts in some other places like a bank or church is considered impolite and should be avoided, if possible. Just look around and see what the locals are wearing and try to match them. As a tourist, the last thing you want to do is stand out in the crowd and attract pickpockets and other unsavory characters.

Tipping

By law, restaurants are supposed to add a 13% tax and 10% tip to your bill. Ticos generally don't bother to add any extra onto the existing tip, so it's by no means expected that you do so. However, if you want to give your server a little more, he or she will likely be most grateful for your generosity.

Hand the tip to them personally and make eye contact with your waiter. It's the polite thing to do.

You should tip your housekeeping staff $1 to $2 a day, depending upon the size of your group. You generally tip each day, not at the end of your stay. They may need the money immediately as most are poor and could use the money immediately.

Interacting With Locals

Ticos are a friendly bunch and dislike the type of tourists who push, rush or talk loudly. Remember, you are in their world – they are not in yours.

It's customary to greet female friends and personal acquaintances with an air kiss on the cheek. The same thing applies when saying goodbye. Men do not kiss men on the cheek. Instead, they shake hands.

In Costa Rica, the word "Gringo" is not negative. It is the way they refer to those who are not from Latin America or Asia. So, if you are referred to as a "gringo" (or "gringa" if you are a woman), don't take offense.

There are complaints about "Gringo pricing" where a Gringo is quoted a higher than the regular price. This sometimes happens when you don't follow proper etiquette in dealing with a Tico.

In every interaction, you are expected to remember your manners and say "Hello" (*Hola!* O-lah) and ask how the person is (*¿Cómo estás?* CO-mo eh-STAHS) - even if you don't know them personally. They will generally respond and ask you how you are: "Good! And you?" (*¡Bueno! Y usted?* BWAY-no EE oo-STED) You can respond in several ways but including "*Pura Vida*" in your response will endear you. Not only are you speaking Spanish, but you are speaking Costa Rica Spanish! Pura Vida is their favorite phrase.

Costa Ricans use "*Con mucho gusto*" ("With much pleasure") instead of "de nada" (it's nothing) which is more commonly used in some other Latin America countries. *Con mucho gusto* is the go-to response when you say thank-you ("*Gracias*").

When you exchange pleasantries on the street, or when walking by a Tico and making eye contact, you can say "Hola!" (Hello) or "Buenas" (BWAY-nas) - a shortened version of "Good morning," or "good afternoon").

If you are trying to get by someone or bump into them accidentally, you can say "perdon" ("perdon" pare-DOAN). You can also say "excuse me" ("¡Disculpe!) Dee-SCHOOL-pay)

Visiting A Tico House

When visiting someone's house it is customary to stand at the gate and shout, *"Upe!"* (OO-pay) to see if anyone is home. To make yourself heard, the word is often extended to "Oooooooooo-paaaaaaaay!" It is a shortened version of Guadalupe, the Virgin Mary, in the Catholic faith. The full phrase that is shortened is *"Ave María purísima, aquí le traigo de parte de nuestra señora la Virgen de Guadalupe."* Presumably, no one with ill intentions would dare utter her name.

If you manage to get someone to come to their fence or gate in front of the house, don't be surprised if you are not invited in. It has nothing to do with being a gringo. Ticos talk through the fence all the time, especially with neighbors. It's a Costa Rica custom that lets the other neighbors know you are not talking about them in private. You'll especially see Tica neighbors carrying on an extended conversation through the locked gate or the fence.

If you are visiting a home where there is no fence or wall, you will need to wait on the street (or sidewalk) until you are greeted. The exception to this is when you have been invited over for coffee or a meal. Under this circumstance, you can approach the house while saying *Upe!* to let the homeowner know you have arrived. Even so, wait for the homeowner to open the door for you. Under no circumstances should you just enter someone's house, even when you have been invited as a guest. In Costa Rica, a person's home is their sanctuary and should be respected and treated as such.

Tico Time

In Costa Rica, anyone arriving within 30-50 minutes of the scheduled time is considered to be on time. This can be the result of traffic or other circumstances.

It's very common for Ticos to arrive late to an event. This is not true for doctor or dentist visits, however. You are expected to be on time.

Ticos don't understand the Gringo habit of being somewhere at the exact minute agreed upon. They refer to it as "*Gringo Ahora*" (GREEN-go uh-OR-ah), or loosely translated as Gringo time.

Bathroom Etiquette

Costa Rica has smaller diameter plumbing than in the U.S. or Europe and so Ticos don't flush toilet paper to avoid jamming the pipe. Used toilet paper is placed in a nearby receptacle. All bathrooms have a wastebasket by the toilet.

Most public bathrooms have signs if they want you to not flush toilet paper.

This is not a hard and fast rule but is true in most Tico homes and businesses. Generally, you'll see a sign in the bathroom (B*año*) advising not to flush tissue.

If you don't know where the bathroom is, ask in Spanish "*¿Dónde está el baño?*" which comes out with the "está el" slurred together and to make it sound like "DON-day eh-STILE BAN-yo?"

You'll see signs for men and women in Spanish that say "*Hombre*" (man) and "*Damas*" (women).

Usually, there's a shared sink to wash your hands outside both bathrooms. Sometimes the women's restroom will have its own sink. It is very common to see incoming customers wash their hands before to sitting down. Ticos are very conscious about cleanliness which shows in their appearance and behaviors.

9 SAFETY

It's important to know how to ask for help. Depending on how urgent your voice sounds, it can range from asking for help in a store or yelling for help in an emergency.

"¡*Ayuda Me!*" (Ah-YOU-dah may)

Some "experts" advise that you should yell "Fire!" (¡*Fuego*! FWAY-goh) in an emergency because it will attract more attention. We've never had to try that one out.

Policía

There are several types of police in Costa Rica. In addition to regular city police (called *La Fuerza Publica*), there are Transitos or traffic police (called *Policia de Transito*}. In addition, there are OIJ police (called *Organismo de Investigacion Judicial)*.

La Fuerza Pública is tasked with crime prevention. OIJ, plainclothes police, oversee criminal investigations. Report the crime to the OIJ police, and if you need victim'sassistance, contact your country's embassy or consulate.

In addition to handing out tickets for traffic violations, Transitos investigate all car accidents. They will also set up checkpoints to make sure your car has the required equipment, and your driver's license and registration are current.

Passport Safety

Your passport is the most valuable thing in your possession while traveling in Costa Rica. Therefore, keep it safe and secure – locked in your hotel safe. Before you lock it away, take a minute to photograph the two pages with your picture and pertinent information on it and the page that has your most current Costa Rica entry stamp.

Keep these photos on your phone wherever you go, in case you are stopped and asked for your passport. The exception is you and your passengers must always have your original passport with you when you're driving.

Where To Keep Your Valuables

For men, it's best to carry your wallet in a front pocket. Pickpockets frequent busy tourist areas.

For women keep your purse on your shoulder with your hand holding onto the strap.

You can also buy leather belts with inside zipper pockets or waist pouches that go on under your clothing. The problem is retrieving money or your passport without attracting attention. The best way we found when using these is to go into a bathroom stall and remove the needed items in privacy.

Prostitution Is Legal

Prostitution is legal in Costa Rica so don't be surprised if you see women looking for gringos in various bars and on some streets. There are several locations in San José and anywhere in Jaco that seem to have an abundance of professional ladies.

Prostitutes in Costa Rica have organized unions, carry medical ID cards, and have police protection. Prostitutes are supposed to be regularly examined by a doctor and are eligible for a no-cost health exam every 15 days if they are registered with *Caja Costarricense de Seguro Social*. CCSS oversees most of Costa Rica's public health sector.

Soliciting sex with a minor is severely punished in Costa Rica. You should also be aware that pimping is illegal (promoting or facilitating the prostitution of another).

Some prostitutes and their associates target gringos for crime, particularly older men. So, if you're retired and a beautiful young Tica shows an interest in you at a bar or on the beach, it's most likely for your money or your valuables or both, and not your engaging personality.

If you want to be safe, it's best to avoid them.

Avoid Sketchy Places

There are sketchy places in most large Costa Rica towns, just as there are in any country. To avoid making yourself a target, avoid those areas.

If you're wondering how to identify sketchy areas, we'll give you a personal example that might help.

We were walking north out of Downtown San José during the middle of the day and quickly noticed a marked decrease in pedestrian traffic on the next block. Instead of walking along with people, we were largely by ourselves. That's when we spotted two scantily dressed women standing on the sidewalk ahead of us, waving to cars going by. We quickly realized we were in a "red-light district" where prostitutes hang out. Instead of turning around, as we should have, we decided to make a block by turning left on the next street and left again on the street after that. Instead of knowing where we were walking, we were walking into uncharted territory.

After stepping over passed-out drunks lying on the sidewalk, we walked by a seedy-looking bar that raised our apprehensions. Thankfully, we didn't attract unwanted attention from a drunk patron who might have seen us.

As we returned to the busier section of town, we were amazed to notice the abrupt transition that we had missed the first time: On one side of the street, people were going about their normal business. On our side, there were few pedestrians and open businesses.

This happened during our first visit to San José and we were not paying as much attention to our surroundings as we should have been.

In smaller towns, the places to avoid are local dive-bars that are away from other local businesses.

A good rule of thumb is if you begin to see graffiti, few people, and a high police presence, this is not where you want to be. Turn around and go back the way you came.

Dial 911 For Emergencies

If you have a cell phone, dial 9-1-1 for emergencies but don't expect a fast response. You may also reach someone who doesn't speak English very well or at all.

In busy tourist areas there are special "Tourist Police" who try to keep an eye on things.

Police in Costa Rica are tasked with preventing crime while the Costa Rica equivalent of the FBI, called the OIJ, investigate crimes. This means even though you contact police about a crime, you must still report it to the OIJ as well.

Crime: Don't Be A Target

Costa Rica is a relatively safe country depending on where you chose to go and when. It's best not to go out walking alone at night. Also, don't walk around with an expensive camera hanging around your neck or on your shoulder. Fancy cell phones, expensive watches, and jewelry make you a target. If you should be accosted, remember none of these items are worth your life. There have been several tourists killed over the years when they resisted giving up their wallets, cellphones, and cameras. Losing your property is not worth losing your life in any country.

You should avoid eating food or drinking a drink that you have left unattended and don't accept a drink from a stranger unless it's handed to you by the bartender. As a matter of safety, you should not leave a bar with a stranger.

You should stay alert in crowded tourist attractions and resort areas popular with foreign tourists.

You should also steer clear of deserted properties or undeveloped land.

Always walk or exercise with a companion. Don't go out walking alone, especially after dark.

While visiting Costa Rica, you should carry a slip of paper with the name and phone number of the hotel where you are staying as well as the phone number of your embassy in Costa Rica. Also, keep the phone numbers for your banks on a separate sheet of paper in case your credit cards or bank cards are stolen or lost.

Beach Safety

Beach safety comes in two parts: you and your possessions. For the beach goer, Costa Rica beaches can be a hazard due to the presence of rip tides or rip currents. **Most beaches don't have lifeguards,** so it is up to you to learn how to spot riptides which are at their strongest from May to November.

Riptides are strong currents that return ocean water from near the beach, back out to the open ocean. You can spot them looking for gaps between the waves. The calmer gap between waves may look safer for you to play without worry about waves washing over your head, but a small patch of calm water in an otherwise choppy sea is often a rip current. You can sometimes see debris floating on top and moving out to sea in the calm water.

IDENTIFYING A RIPTIDE:

Riptides won't pull you under, but they will pull you out to sea, away from the beach. They are too strong to swim against, but you can swim parallel to the beach to escape the current.

If you can't escape the current, wave an arm to attract attention on the beach. Then, it's just a matter of staying afloat until help reaches you.

The other part of beach safety is taking precautions with your valuables, such as wallets, watches and cell phones. Bring a resealable plastic bag, such as a Ziploc, to store your valuables and keep them from getting wet. It's best if you make this transfer in the car when no one is looking rather than on the beach, surrounded by people.

Don't leave the plastic bag on your towel. Bury it in the sand where you are sitting. You can do this somewhat inconspicuously by sitting on the top part of your beach towel and pulling the bottom part up between your legs. You then dig the hole between your legs, put your plastic bag in the hole, covering it back up and placing the bottom of your towel over the covered hole. Sure, a thief could dig it up while you're out in the water but by making it that much harder, you've gained precious seconds you need to respond, if you see someone sketchy moving your towel. Most petty crimes are those of opportunity. If it's too time-consuming or too much trouble to locate valuables, the thief will move on to an easier situation.

The last thing most Costa Ricans want is a reputation as an unsafe destination for tourists. As a result, there have been instances on thefts on tourist beaches where local Ticos have chased down and caught thieves who were targeting tourists.

Pedestrian Right-Of-Way

If you are walking and crossing a street, be very careful, because pedestrians do not have the right of way in Costa Rica. Don't step in front of an oncoming car, expecting it to stop. Be especially wary of fast motorcycles headed your way. A good rule of thumb is to watch the locals and cross when they do.

Yes, You Can Drink The Water

Speaking of safety, tap water is perfectly safe in almost all of Costa Rica.

In Latin America, there are only two countries were drinking tap water is safe, one of them is Costa Rica, and the other one is Chile.

Even though the water is safe to drink, there are a few places, like the Caribbean Coast where it not advisable, due to the taste. If you are in one of the rare places where the water is not potable, there will be plenty of signs to let you know. Bottled water is cheap and available everywhere.

When you are in a tourist area, be sure to ask for a glass of water ("*Vaso de agua*" VAH-so day AHG-wah). Otherwise, you may be given a bottle of water and be charged for it.

If you want ice in it, ask for a glass of water with ice ("*Vaso de agua con hielo*" VAH-so day AHG-wah cone yel-low). And don't forget to follow with a "please" (por fah-VOR).

10 SPEAKING THE LANGUAGE

Even if you only know a few words in Spanish, use them as often as possible. Ticos will appreciate your effort and respond in kind.

We've found many Ticos speak at least a little English but will sometimes say they don't because they either don't want to be embarrassed by making a mistake or they just want to find out what you have to say about them and their country when you think they don't understand what you're saying..

During our time here, we've made friends with Ticos and Ticas who at first told us they didn't know English but started speaking English after we became friends.

A better idea would be to brush up on your Spanish before making the trip. Speaking and understanding Spanish will open more opportunities for you during your visit, both financially and making friends.

If you ever find yourself at a loss for words, the phrase *"Pura Vida"* (poor ah-VEE-dah) will save the day. The phrase is used in place of hello, goodbye, great, and in answer to the question "How are you doing?"

Even if you don't understand a word of what someone tells you, a friendly "Pura Vida" in reply will help. It is the go-to phrase in Costa Rica. Add the Tico slang word *"mae"* (pronounced my) and you're all set: *"Pura Vida, mae!"* Mae means "Mate", "dude", "bro", "guy".

¡Qué *lindo/bonito!* (kay LEEN-doh/boh-NEE-toh) means "How beautiful! This phrase can be used for everything from a view to a dog to a baby.

"Suave un toque" (SWA-ve oon TOK-ey) This phrase means "wait" "slow down" or even the English phrase "hold your horses"! Ticos also say this when things are getting heated and they want someone to relax. *"Suave mae!"* means "chill out", "calm down" or "relax". "Tranquilo (tran-KEE-low) can also be used, as it has basically the same meaning.

Al chile (ah CHEE-lay) is used in place of *"Verdad,"* as in "Really?" The literal translation is "to the Chile" which has no relation to the real meaning.

Jamal (juh-MALL) can replace comer ("co-MER) to say "to eat."

Speaking of eating, ¡Qué *rico! (KAY REE-coh)* Means "How delicious!" (literally translated as "How rich!"

11 AIRPORT FORMALITIES

The San José Airport (airport code SJO) is not in San José, it's in Alajuela – the second largest city in Costa Rica.

The closest hotel to the airport is the Courtyard by Marriott, about 1/2 mile from the airport (walkable, down the side of a major road). The hotel is next to a Walmart Supercenter and across from several casual patio restaurants (also an iPhone store). It is less than a half-mile to City Mall, the largest shopping mall in Central America (continuing down the same major road, with a crossover underneath the road at the mall). If you have an early morning flight, this is your best bet for staying close to the airport.

Almost as close are the Hampton Inn and Holiday Inn Express, but they are not easily walkable or as close to the mall. Both are next to a Denny's.

While the major taxis are red, the only taxis that can pick up in the airport are orange. The orange taxis pay an extra fee for airport access and that is reflected in their fares. If you have a long distance to go from the airport, you can save money by walking out of the airport building and turning left, walking along the sidewalk, against one-way traffic. Make a right on the busy one-way toward the covered bus stops. You'll see red taxis parked in a line across the street. There's usually a guy along the area you walk who solicits for the red taxis. (See more in the "Taxi Formalities" section).

The actual name of the "San José" airport is the Juan Santamaria International Airport, named after a young Costa Rican soldier. The army drummer gave his life in a decisive battle against a U.S. mercenary who tried to overtake the country with his private army in 1856. It's quite a story and there's a large statue of Santamaria in a park named after him in nearby downtown Alajuela, his hometown.

From Landing To Exit At SJO

You'll be asked to fill out a customs form while in flight, before landing in Costa Rica. This will include your passport information. This is also where you will need to declare anything you are bringing into the country, such as pharmaceuticals.

When you exit the plane, you'll go first through immigration and then customs.

The immigration officer will ask you what your business is in the country and how long you will be here. The magic number is 90 days ("noventa días" no-VENTA DEE-ahs). That is the longest the immigration officer is allowed by law to give you. The number of days he writes on the passport stamp is totally at his or her discretion, even if you have a return ticket stating otherwise. It's best to smile, be polite and hope for the best.

Leaving immigration, you'll go down a hallway and through a very large duty-free area on your way to the baggage claim. Imported alcohol and wine is expensive in Costa Rica so it's best to buy it here without the added taxes. You're allowed to bring in up to 5 liters per person (18 and over).

ATMs are in the main airport lobby, in baggage claim and beside gates 2 and 6. There is also a BAC (Bank of San José) branch in the lobby where withdrawals can be made in colones, US Dollars, and Euros. There are also money exchange locations along your route out of the airport. As discussed earlier, it is not recommended you use these as the fees and exchange rate are higher than you will find once outside the airport.

If you want to get through customs as quickly as possible, grab a Skycap porter. They'll be standing together as you enter the baggage area. Even if you have only one bag, grab a porter. You'll thank us later.

The porter, who may or may not speak English, will ask for your baggage ticket and will stand with you at the carousel to wait for your bag. It's best if you can tell the porter what color your bag is. You'll need to know the color in Spanish if they don't speak English. An even better idea is to take photos of your bags on your cellphone so you can show the porter what your bags look like.

When you motion toward your bag, the porter will grab it and place it on the cart, and you follow him to customs. You'll see a long line of people in customs, waiting to go through the x-ray scanning machine. The porters have their own line to the left and will hand your form to the customs official and place your bag on the conveyor belt to be X-rayed. After that, they will put it back on the cart and you follow them out to the street where you'll be bombarded with multiple drivers yelling "Taxi?" and shuttle drivers holding signs with customer names or destinations. If you've ordered a shuttle or private driver, this is where you need to read all the signs, in order to find the driver holding a sign with your name on it.

The porter will take your bag to the vehicle and you pay him then. There is no set fee, but we usually pay from $3 -$4 (2 – 5 mil), depending on how many bags and how far they take them. If you have someone picking you up and they are in the parking garage, the porter will take your bags to the car.

Beware of "helpers" who sometimes show up as you leave the airport building and try to take any bag you are pulling or carrying. They try to appear like they are part of the porter service, but they aren't. Never let anyone besides the porter or taxi driver handle your bag.

If you are going to a hotel near the airport, the orange airport taxis are fine. We have had orange taxis refuse to take us the short distance, in favor of waiting for passengers who are going further, so be aware.

From here, you have a choice of paying the meter rate or, if it's a long drive, you can negotiate the price. Make sure the meter (called a "Maria") is on and started. If there's already a fare on the meter, tell the driver to restart the meter ("ponga la Maria, por favor"). On occasion, you will come across a taxi driver who pretends not to hear or understand you. If they refuse to reset the meter, tell them to stop (alto). This usually results in the meter being reset.

Remember, the commonly referred-to "San José Airport" is not in San José, it's in Alajuela. If you have a place booked in San José and want to take a taxi, make like a Tico and say "Chepe" (CHE pay) which is slang for José.

You can also catch an Uber at the airport but it's best to avoid meeting in an area where there are taxis since the two are at odds in Costa Rica. Either go upstairs to Airport Arrivals and summon an Uber with the app or walk down to the bus stop area and summon from there. Keep in mind, Uber only serves Alajuela, San José, Heredia, and Cartago for now. Uber is not currently officially recognized by Costa Rica and the regular taxi drivers resent Uber to the point that some Uber drivers have been assaulted and their personal cars damaged. Uber is in negotiations with the Costa Rican government but, even if their presence is sanctioned, they are taking money out of the pockets of regular taxi drivers and the resentment is not likely to go away.

Flying From San José

Be sure to check in online for your flight 24 hours before your flight leaves.

It's best to plan to arrive 2 hours before your international flight, to allow for any traffic or airport delays you may encounter before your flight.

Departure fees from Costa Rica are now included by almost all airlines, so there is no need to pay separately at the airport.

You must be checked in and holding a boarding pass, with your bags checked at least one hour before international departure. If you miss this deadline, you risk being turned away.

Once you have checked in and have your boarding pass, you'll proceed to the security line (to your left as you enter the airport). There, you'll have to remove metal objects and step through a metal detector. As always, keep an eye on your stuff after you place it on the conveyor belt to make sure no one picks up something of yours by mistake.

After that, you proceed into the departure level of the airport, filled with lots of expensive shops. If you have any leftover Colones, this is a great place to get rid of them. There's also a duty-free shop.

If you are flying First or Business Class on an airline that is a member of the Star Alliance, you are welcome to enter the Copa Club Lounge on the departure level of the airport. Just look for the signs. You can also pay $50 for a day pass – worth it if you have a long wait for your plane. There are Copa Club lounges at both San José (Juan Santamaria Airport) and the Liberia Airport. Flying First or Business Class also entitles you to use the fast track lane through security located on the far right as you look at the security area.

The Liberia Airport

The Daniel Oduber Quiros International Airport (airport code LIR) is located 12 km west of the city of Liberia in Guanacaste Province.

This is the airport you should fly into or out of if you are going to any Guanacaste beach towns, such as Tamarindo, Playa Hermosa, Playas de Coco, and Playa Flamingo areas. An added advantage of going through the Liberia airport is that it is much smaller, so it only takes about 20-30 minutes to clear immigration and customs. The airport began 24-hour operations in 2019.

The distance between the Liberia, Costa Rica Airport and the San José Airport is approximately 210 km or about 130 miles (approximately 4-5 hours driving time). The 4-5 hour driving time is not a typo – it is the reality of driving in Costa Rica (as discussed above).

There are non-stop flights to the airport from many major U.S. cities including New York, Miami, Atlanta, Houston, and Los

Angeles. Make sure you buy a ticket to Liberia, Costa Rica and not Liberia in Africa!

You will find shared shuttles to many of the major beach towns. Taxis are also available, but they are the most expensive option. The bus that serves the airport will take you into Liberia and from there you could transfer to a bus going to your destination. Rental cars are also available.

If you need a hotel close to the airport, the Hilton Garden Inn is just across the road from the terminal. A less expensive option is the Hotel Santa Anna, 2 km west of the airport.

Domestic Airlines

Sansa Air flies to 12 destinations in the country: San José, Liberia, La Fortuna/Arenal, Puerto Jiménez, Golfito, Palmar Sur, Drake Bay, Quepos/Manuel Antonio, Tambor, Tamarindo, Limon and Tortuguero.

Sansa uses smaller planes than the major international airlines, so they have weight restrictions. Currently, restrictions are 20 – 30 pounds (11- 13 kilograms). This is important to keep in mind if you are transferring from an international flight to a domestic flight. You may not be able to take all your luggage, due to weight restrictions on the smaller planes.

Don't Buy Souvenirs At The Airport

Like most airports, shops at San José and Liberia airports have items for sale that are extremely overpriced.

Souvenirs are also more expensive at the airport stores. There is no shortage of souvenir shops wherever tourists are found in Costa Rica. You will save a lot of money by buying where you visit rather than waiting until you are leaving to get gifts for family and friends.

If you're bringing coffee back from Costa Rica, you'll save money by buying it at a grocery store instead of the airport. For Costa Rica liquor, there are duty-free shops inside the departure and arrival terminals.

12 HIRING A PRIVATE DRIVER

Hiring your own private, English-speaking driver in Costa Rica is a smart and easy way to see the country while on vacation. Not only will the driver take care of all the driving, but he'll also know more about the route and destination than you do, so you'll have the added benefit of learning things along the way and get tips on where you are headed.

A good driver will engage you during the trip and point out sights along the way that you might have driven right by. He's also on YOUR schedule so you can stop wherever you want and add destinations to your trip.

We have a dependable driver that we've used for years and he has become a close family friend to us. Perhaps you'll have a similar experience.

Finding A Private Driver

Join one of the numerous Costa Rica Expat groups on Facebook and ask for recommendations. Be forewarned, there are a lot of sarcastic, know-it-alls on these groups who will also respond. It's best just to ignore their comments. Try Quora.com if you're not on Facebook.

By identifying a driver with recommendations, you're already verifying the credentials of the person. Respond only to people recommending drivers – not actual posts directly from drivers.

Remember, anyone can call themselves a private driver. It is not regulated in Costa Rica. The only thing you must go on is a recommendation from someone else. Good drivers have many people recommending them.

Negotiating With A Private Driver

You should pay per trip – not by the hour or kilometer. That said, you should also agree on the amount of time the driver will be available. You don't want to hire a driver at 8 am. and find out he has another customer scheduled at 2 pm. so he'll have to drop you off by then.

As we mention, travel times in Costa Rica vary greatly and are frequently long, due to traffic delays and closed roads. This is why distances are often given by time rather than in kilometers. Your cost should be a flat rate, not dependent on what time you arrive.

If you stop for a meal, you are under no obligation to purchase a meal for the driver. However, if you stop at a "Soda" where meals are not that expensive it might behoove you to include the driver. That way you can discuss the trip over a meal. Use it as an opportunity to gain even more knowledge about where you are going or thinking of going next.

Private drivers are used to very late night and very early morning plane arrivals and departures so don't worry about asking to be picked up at 3 am. for a 6 am. departure. Better yet, tell them what time you need to be at the airport and let them decide when you should be picked up.

13 RENTAL CAR FORMALITIES

A Caution About Renting

Renting a car sometimes goes without much thought when visiting a foreign country, but it shouldn't.

In Costa Rica driving a car comes with added perils and pitfalls. For example, bad drivers and road dangers are the norms in Costa Rica. Even though a license is required to drive on Costa Rica roads, people who have flunked the driver's test can sometimes pay the examiner to "help" them obtain a valid license.

I have often compared driving in Costa Rica to "driving" on a video game obstacle course where dangerous things pop out in front of you at the most inopportune times. It is like that driving here every day. Is that the way you really want to spend part of your vacation? If you spend five days at a resort, do you want to be paying for a rental car the entire time when you could easily take a bus or grab a cheap taxi?

A lot of Costa Rica tourism sites and blogs promote special deals with rental car companies (see below) but we have yet to see one blog that advocates not renting.

You're coming to Costa Rica to experience the "Pura Vida" and shouldn't get uptight unnecessarily while on vacation. That's why we suggest you consider taking the bus and/or hiring an English-speaking driver for your travels in Costa Rica.

Traffic accidents are one of the leading causes of death in Costa Rica. This figure only includes those where the death occurs at the accident scene, not when death occurs on the way to the hospital or at the hospital. Being in a traffic accident where someone is seriously injured or killed can have its own set of pitfalls, including you being prohibited from leaving the country until all matters regarding the accident (including recovering from injuries) have been resolved.

If you're on a budget, the biggest problem with renting is the hidden cost tacked onto to your rental quote. This includes mandatory insurance and putting a hold of $1,000 to $1,500 USD on your credit or debit card if you don't get maximum coverage. The insurance cost could easily double your "quote."

You can drive with a foreign driver's license for up to three months as a tourist, so there is no need to get an international drivers' license before you come.

Rental Car Tips

When most people in the United States think of rental car companies, they think of Hertz, Avis, Budget or Alamo. You'll find those companies in Costa Rica but the largest rental car company here is locally-based Adobe.

Since Adobe is a Costa Rica rental car company they know everything there is to know about car rentals in the country. They have the most offices in Costa Rica, which is a major selling point if you end up with car trouble somewhere far from the airport.

Adobe has a modern fleet of cars and has no hidden fees – another plus.

Some Costa Rica blogs have a discount deal with Adobe, which you should take advantage of, rather than booking directly off the Adobe website. Our favorite is My Tan Feet, which offers up to 20 percent off and a bunch of free extras, like adding an extra driver.

Don't rely on your credit card's rental car coverage in Costa Rica. Costa Rica requires that the rental car be covered for liability for damage to property and people other than the rented car. This is separate from what your credit card company covers.

Some rental companies here may not accept credit card coverage anyway.

Pay for insurance coverage here and pay for full coverage, if you can afford it. With it, you will be covered for any and all damage to your rental car. Costa Rica roads can be treacherous and very hard on a car, due to numerous potholes and debris in the road. Without full coverage, you could be hit with hundreds of dollars in tire damage after you turn your car back in. Keep in mind, it can be expensive, but it may be worth it for the peace of mind you'll have on a worry-free vacation here.

You don't need four-wheel drive unless you are planning on going someplace remote and off the beaten path.

If you rent a car from the San José airport location, there will be a hefty surcharge. To reduce that cost, try to rent away from the airport (being sure to return it to the same location when you're through). For example, the Alajuela Adobe location is just a short, 5-minute ride from the airport and Adobe provides a free airport shuttle. You can find all their locations in Costa Rica on their website.

Note: We did not get any commission or fee from Adobe for our endorsement.

Follow your rental car company's advice and directions on what to do and who to call if you are involved in an accident.

GPS?

While using your personal cell phone is fine for in-town driving, you may drive through areas that don't have cell phone coverage. That means you'll lose your cell phone GPS map. A way around this is to either download the maps to your phone before you leave cell phone coverage or rent a GPS for your car in Costa Rica.

Carry Your Passport

Costa Rica law requires that you have your passport with you when you drive. If the Transitos stop you and you don't have it, you may have to leave the car where they stopped you and get your passport. The law has been updated so that regular police can also stop you and that all passengers in the vehicle must have their passports with them as well.

Some expats say a color copy of your passport will work instead. We have not been able to test the validity of this claim. If you want to try this, you should have a color copy of your identification page and of your entry stamp page with your entry stamp. They need that to determine if you are in the country during the allotted time on your entry stamp (usually 90 days are given, but it's up to the discretion of the immigration officer when you arrive in the country).

You should consider buying a security pocket that hangs around your neck. You can keep your passport, credit cards and money in it underneath your shirt.

Tico Drivers And Roads

Tico drivers are creative and passive aggressive. If you plan to drive a rental car in Costa Rica, you must always be alert for the unexpected.

You'll find cars on the wrong side of the road, trying to get past a traffic jam and turning unexpectedly from any lane, without using a turn signal.

Tico drivers will also stop in the traffic lane to talk to someone on the side of the road or use their cell phone while they have a good cell phone signal. Oftentimes they don't turn on their emergency flashers or turn signals to indicate they are stopped or about to turn.

Speed bumps, called "muertos" (dead people). The name started as "policía muerto", a dead policeman and Ticos shortened it over time. This is an important expression to know because they are everywhere, and the size of them isn't regulated. Some are makeshift and can be very large. Many are also not painted yellow and don't come with a yellow warning sign preceding them. It's best not to come to a full stop when approaching them as you may get rear-ended by the driver behind you who is texting while driving.

Many bridges are single lane but usually have a "yield" sign (Ceda el Paso) on one side. If you see the sign on your side, you must wait for traffic coming from the other direction to cross the bridge. Some bridges have speed bumps on each end of the bridge.

If a driver blinks his headlights twice for you, it usually means you can go ahead, or make a turn.

Stop signs and even stop lights are considered "suggestions" by many Tico drivers. Don't be surprised to see a car pull into traffic even though you have a green light and they have a red.

Be especially alert on two-lane mountain roads for weaving oncoming traffic that may cross the center line into your lane.

Many Tico drivers will attempt to pass slow vehicles even on a double-yellow line.

Motorcycles are everywhere in Costa Rica and they make a habit of lane splitting (it's not illegal here). Be alert for motorcycles on any side of your car and for motorcycles to suddenly drive onto the roadway in front of you.

Motorized bicycles are also popular in Costa Rica. Be prepared. They don't follow traffic laws and can pop out of anywhere.

Now, the good news…

Tico drivers can also be incredibly helpful if you run into trouble on the road. We know one Gringo who had a flat tire on the way to the beach. His spare was also flat (it was his personal car). A Tico driver stopped, lent him his own spare and told him to drop it off at a car repair shop on the outskirts of the town he was going to. The Tico who owned the repair shop was a friend of the good Samaritan.

We've heard similar stories from other Gringo friends who say Ticos have stopped to help then when they had difficulties on the side of the road.

Don't Drive At Night

It gets dark around 6 pm. year-round in Costa Rica, so you should plan to arrive at your destination by then.

Absolutely do not drive at night in Costa Rica. There are too many hazards on the roads that you won't see until it's too late. Also, many roads are not well marked, there are no shoulders and few signs. This is very important if you are arriving late in the afternoon or during the night. Stay safe and book a hotel close to the airport, then wait to rent a car the next morning.

Do you really want to risk breaking down or immobilizing your car in a crash on a dark road in the middle of nowhere in a foreign country? Driving at night is just not worth it.

'Parking Lot Full' Scam

When approaching a major tourist area with public parking, be aware of the "parking lot full" scam.

For example, if you are driving to the entrance of Manuel Antonio Park, there are several parking lots adjacent to the

park. (By parking lots, we mean grass-covered fields). It is common for the attendants of parking lots a little further away to tell drivers going past them that the parking lot ahead is full, and the drivers need to pull into their parking lot. Don't fall for it. There's nothing to stop you from driving past them to see for yourself and then coming back if the closer lots are full.

Rental Car Safety

Make sure you put your luggage in the trunk and never leave anything in the car when you are away from it. Thieves can spot rental cars by license plate (placa) and are known to target them.

If you are stuck in a traffic backup, don't allow your passengers to hold anything valuable in their laps when the windows are down. We've seen dash cam videos of thieves walking up from behind on the passenger side, grabbing a purse or phone from the unwary passenger and then darting across stopped lanes of traffic to hop on a motorcycle that speeds away.

Even people panhandling have been known to lean in to ask for money and then snatch a phone from a dash mount, running away before anyone can get out of the car.

Gas (Petrol) Stations

When filling up at the gas station, you do not get out and pump your own gas, because all stations are full service.

You can buy gas either by asking the attendant to "fill it up" or requesting a certain amount in Colones.

To fill it up, you say "*Lleno*" (JEY-no) followed by "*regular*" (reg-you-LAR) or for premium, you say "*Lleno Super*" (JEY-no SOOP-er). To pay only a certain amount say the amount in Colones (Un mil, Dos mil, tres mil, cuatro mil, cinco mil, and so forth. Remember a "mil" is 1,000 Colones, not a million.

You can ask your attendant to clean your windshield, check the air in your tires, and check the oil. Some attendants may do the first two without your asking.

The attendant will tell you the price, but you can also look at the pump if you don't understand him. The top number is the price and bottom number is the number of liters.

The price of gas is set by the government and is the same at every gas station in Costa Rica. Gas is priced by the liter.

14   TAXI FORMALITIES

Make sure the taxi meter (called a "Maria") is on and started. If there's already a fare on the meter larger than 650 or 750, tell the driver to restart the meter ("*ponga la Maria, por favor*").

Always have small change for the taxi (nothing larger than a 10-mil (10,000 colones), preferably a 5, some 2's and some 1's. It's best to avoid giving them a 10-mil if you have a fare that's below 5 mil. In some cases, they'll say they don't have change and try to keep your 10.

Taxi fares are based on time as well as revolutions of the car wheels. If your driver is going back and forth between a short distance, they are trying to run up the meter. Another trick is to drive the long way around a parking lot to increase the fare. If possible, have the driver drop you on the road in front of your destination, rather than through the parking lot to the door.

You don't need to tip a taxi driver as it is not customary. But, if you and your taxi driver got along and you got some good information from them about something, it would be a nice gesture to round-up your fare (for instance, the fare is 6,200 colones, give them a 10 and ask for 3,000 change ("*tres mil, por favor*"). You should also round up if the ride is so short the meter didn't hit 1,000 colones.

'Door Slammers'

Tourists from the United States have a reputation among taxi drivers as "door slammers." Taxi drivers are very proud of their cars and take very good care of them. One thing they absolutely hate is for passengers to slam the door when getting in and out. Do them and favor and shut the taxi door gently. They'll appreciate it.

Red Taxis vs. Piratas

Red Taxis are the official taxis in Costa Rica. They are red with a yellow light on top and a yellow triangle sticker on the door. The name of the town in which they operate is in the yellow triangle. They are licensed and fully insured, and the taxis are well kept and clean.

Other taxis are referred to as pirate taxis ("taxis piratas" or just "piratas"). They sometimes charge less and may or may not have a meter. If there is no meter, be sure to agree on a price for your destination before you start your ride. You can negotiate the fare with these taxi drivers, but keep in mind if they are involved in an accident where you are injured, they may or may not have insurance.

One way to save money on a taxi, if you are going to be around a few days, is to talk to the taxi driver. Many of them speak English. When you get to your destination, ask for their card. Don't be afraid to ask them what they would charge to a certain destination. Then, when you need a taxi, call the number on the card instead of the number for the taxi company.

Most towns have locations around the central park and bus stations where taxis wait for fares. Otherwise, the staff at the hotel or restaurant can call a taxi for you. In addition to four-door sedans, vans with wheelchair lifts, and trucks are also available depending upon where you are going and what your needs are.

15   BUS FORMALITIES

Buses in Costa Rica are cheap ("barato" buh-RAH-tow) but they are time consuming because of the stops they make along the way. For that reason, you shouldn't take the bus on a two- or three-day visit. It will waste too much time.

A bus stop is called "*La parada*" (lah puh-RAH-dah) and can be marked with a small sheltered bench and/or with a yellow rectangle painted on the street (for local routes). If you see one on the opposite side of the street, the stop for a bus going the other way would be directly across from it. As the bus approaches, you extend your arm to let the driver know you want him to stop.

Buses have their destination visible in the front window – either on a placard or in an electronic sign.

Inside the bus, there are either long strings or red buttons to alert the bus driver that a stop is requested.

You won't find "chicken buses" in Costa Rica, but you will find old school buses used for a few local neighborhood routes. Except for service animals, the presence of animals on buses is prohibited by law. There are two types of bus routes here: inter-city and intra-city. Almost always, they use different terminals.

For city bus service, look for the fare posted on the bottom left of the front window. The fare is also displayed inside the bus near the driver. If you are not going to the destination, tell the bus driver the barrio (neighborhood) where you will be getting off. You may pay a lower fare that way. When in doubt, give the bus driver one or two mil. You should pay in Colones. Many bus drivers will not accept dollars. The drivers will give you change if you don't have the exact fare. They do appreciate the exact fare and smaller bills.

Be sure and don't stop on the entrance step with the yellow rectangular poles. These devices count the number of passengers going past them. If you stop on the step, the bus driver will tell you to move. You may also hear it beeping if you stop on it.

For intra-city bus service, it's wise to purchase bus tickets in advance, if you are going to a popular destination. Even buying a ticket an hour or two early is preferable to waiting until the last minute. You'll receive a ticket with a number on it and this is your assigned seat. The seats are numbered starting from the front. Intra-city buses are on par with buses throughout North America and Europe.

Two Types Of Buses

There are two types of inter-city buses: direct ("directo") and collectives ("colectivo").

Direct buses travel from one destination to the next with few or no stops. Think of them as "express" buses. The collective buses make more stops, collecting people along the highway and dropping people off. As a result, they are much slower getting to their destination. They are also cheaper. Always compare the travel ti mes to find the fastest bus.

Bus drivers will stop to pick up passengers even when all the seats are filled. That means you might end up standing if you board an inter-city bus without a ticket.

Some routes require multiple bus changes, such as Grecia to La Fortuna. You catch the Naranjo bus coming from Alajuela in Grecia. Getting off in Naranjo, you then must catch either a La Fortuna bus or a San Carlos bus. The San Carlos bus goes through San Carlos and ends in nearby Quesada, at a major bus terminal. From Quesada, you would then catch a third bus to La Fortuna.

You pay for each leg when you get on the bus since the buses are usually not the same bus line. Tell the driver your destination when boarding so he can determine your fare.

Another thing we learned in traveling to a destination: if the bus driver gives you what looks like a business card when you board, hold on to it. When he makes a pit stop and everyone leaves, you need to show the card to re-board the bus. Not all bus drivers do that.

For bus terminology in Costa Rica, refer to the Appendix.

Always Be Vigilant

Keep an eye on your backpacks and luggage when riding buses. There are overhead racks on most buses. We suggest you place your backpack on the rack across from where you are sitting so you can keep an eye on it. We also suggest you leave a strap hanging down to remind you to grab your backpack when you leave the bus.

For inter-city buses, there should be an assistant who will take your luggage and place it underneath, freeing the driver to take tickets at the door. If possible, sit on the side of the bus that your luggage was placed in, so you can keep an eye on it as people exit the bus along the route and pull their bag from the luggage compartment.

Be watchful for luggage thieves. They target buses that go to and from popular tourist destinations. If anything happens on a bus to distract you (like a woman in front of you dropping her change), keep a close eye on your belongings. This is a common trick for the unsuspecting tourist.

Finding The Correct Bus Terminal

There are many bus terminals in San José. Each can represent a bus company or several bus companies. You can go anywhere in the country by bus from San José. You just must find the right terminal and the bus schedule.

For popular routes, it is possible to buy your bus ticket at the terminal several days in advance. You go to the ticket window and tell them where you want to go, what day and what time. Some bus companies also sell tickets online.

A great resource for finding your way by bus in Costa Rica is "Costa Rica By Bus" (a Facebook page).

16   TAXI OR BUS ALTERNATIVES

A good option for a taxi or bus is Interbus. It's a shuttle service that runs vans between main tourist areas in Costa Rica. Interbus will pick you up at your hotel or the airport and take you to your destination. Some routes require changing shuttles.

There are many other shuttle services operating in Costa Rica. Check with your hotel for recommendations.

There are also private drivers available that provide chauffeur service between destinations. The added advantage of a private driver (if they speak English) is that you can learn a lot from them during the trip. They will point out interesting places and answer your questions as you travel.

You can get recommendations for private drivers on TripAdvisor.com or on any of the many Costa Rica Facebook groups that cater to expats.

17   DIRECTIONS IN COSTA RICA

Costa Rica is famous for not having street addresses or even street names in many cases. You may see streets labeled on Google maps, but many of those names aren't used practically. Instead of an address (dirección), directions are used, such as "*Arriba Cajon, 300 metros después de la Iglesia, Casa Verde con techo rojo a la izquierda,*" which would be "Above Cajon, 3 blocks past the church green house with a red roof on the left." Directions are usually given from a known point – a church, school, park, or business — in a rough measurement (estimating distance).

A quirk of the country is that some directions start from a point that was around in the past but is no longer there (a tree or a business). In San José, one of the bus terminals is called "The Coca Cola," even though the Coca Cola plant it was next to has been gone for years.

When you visit Costa Rica, directions to your hotel may come in this manner. In Spanish (Español), the compass directions are Norte, Este, Sur, and Oeste.

It's helpful to know that almost all Catholic churches in Costa Rica face west. Many addresses in Costa Rica are based on distance and direction from those churches. It's so parishioners sit facing east, toward Jerusalem and the place of crucifixion.

Just find a church with a park in front of it and chances are it faces west.

Understanding Distance In Meters

The easiest way to understand short distances in meters is to remember that 100 meters is about one block (*una cuadra* OO-nah KWAD-rah). So, if the directions are 200 meters west (*Oeste*) and

100 meters north (*Norte*), that means its two blocks west and then go one block north. This does not mean that all blocks are 100 meters long.

The easy way to convert miles to kilometers is by looking at the speedometer in your Costa Rica rental car. The next easiest is by percentage. To convert a mile to a kilometer, you're adding 60% to the number. While that's kind of hard to do in your head, if you break it down into the number + 50% + 10% (60%), it makes it much easier. For example, 50 miles = 50+25+5 or 80 kilometers. (The precise conversion is 80.4672)

To convert kilometers to miles, you do the opposite: subtract 40%. Again, it's much easier if you break it down. (Subtract 50%, then add 10% back.) For example, converting 120 km to miles: 120 – 60 + 12 (100% - 50% + 10%) It comes out to 72. The exact measurement is 74.5645. Not quite as accurate as miles to kilometers, but it still gives you a close estimate.

18 MONEY & EXPENSES

In many other Latin American countries, the Peso is the name for money. The Spanish word for Columbus is Colon, and Costa Rica honored Christopher Columbus by naming its money after him.

The smallest denomination of paper money in circulation in Costa Rica is the 1,000 colones bill ("*un mil*" OON mill). The next highest is the 2,000 colones bill ("*dos mil*" DOSE mill). After that, there is the 5,000 colones bill ("*cinco mil*" SEEN-coh mill), the 10,000 colones bill ("*diez mil*" de-EZ mill), and the 20,000 colones bill ("*vente mil*

BEN-tee mill). Exchange rates vary, and it is a good idea to check what it is before arriving.

Counterfeiting is a problem in Costa Rica, so expect the cashier (*caja* CAH ha) to examine any 10 or 20-mil bill you give them. It's not because you look suspicious, but tourists are the easiest "mark" to pass a counterfeit bill to since they are likely unfamiliar with the currency. At places like restaurants and pharmacies, you will see signs saying "Caja, " which is the location where you pay for your purchases.

The largest coin in general circulation is 500 Colones. The next are the 100, 50, 25, 10 and 5 Colones coins. Try to use small bills and coins when dealing with street vendors and smaller businesses, especially early in the day. In other words, don't use a 20 mil note to pay for something that costs two mil.

Torn Bills

Be aware that torn bills – either Colones or dollars – will probably not be accepted by most businesses. Torn bills are considered "broken." Torn bills will usually have to be taken to the bank and exchanged for bills without a tear.

Money Exchanges

Avoid changing money at the airport because the exchange rates are high. This also goes for manned currency exchange booths at the airport. U.S. dollars are accepted as easily as colons (in most areas) but you are at the mercy of the person you are giving your dollars to, for a good exchange rate.

Pay Cash, If Possible

Cash is king in Costa Rica and many businesses will give a discount, if asked, for paying cash ("efectivo" e-fec-TIVO). This is especially true in pharmacies.

If you prefer to use a credit card, make sure it's from an institution that does not charge an international transaction fee. Also, remember to notify your credit card company that you will be on vacation in Costa Rica, so your card doesn't get flagged as possibly stolen.

We suggest uslng a debit card to withdraw cash at ATMs in colones. Always withdraw the maximum available instead of smaller amounts more often, as you will pay a set ATM fee (to the Costa Rica bank) every time you use it. Don't carry all your cash with you. Leave what you don't need in your hotel safe or in a safe place in your room.

When using an ATM make sure you stay on top of the transaction. Waiting even a few extra seconds to take your card out the machine can result in the machine confiscating your card. The ATMs are programmed to do this in the event you left your card in the machine by accident and to prevent the person behind you from using your card. Always use an ATM which is attached (inside or beside) a bank. Freestanding ATMs can belong to any one of several banks and if your card is confiscated by the machine, it can be quite complicated to determine which bank owns the machine. Also, it will take longer for a confiscated card to be returned to the bank which owns the machine. In the event your card is confiscated by the machine, immediately go into the bank and explain what has happened. They will tell you when confiscated cards are retrieved from the machines to be returned to the owners. Keep in mind, this can take several days which is why we always withdraw the maximum amount allowed so if things go south, we have cash in hand. To retrieve your ATM card, you will need to return to the bank where it was confiscated on the day you are told and be sure to bring your passport.

Any transactions done in a bank, including breaking down larger denomination bills to smaller ones will require a passport. This is primarily due to money laundering and counterfeit issues. Also, when entering a bank, you will be required to remove any hat or sunglasses. This is so the security cameras can get a good look at you should you decide to rob the bank.

Spend All Your Colones

You should try to spend all your colones before you leave the country. Don't bring a large sum back with you. It's a hassle trying to convert colones back to dollars when you get home and you'll get hit by the exchange rate again. The same goes for airport money exchanges.

Try to use U.S. dollars during your last day or two. Spend your colones in Costa Rica and leave with dollars in your pocket.

Traveler's Checks

It's best to avoid bringing Travelers Checks to Costa Rica as there are few places in Costa Rica that accept them.

19 USING YOUR CELL PHONE

If you have a smartphone, it's a good idea to load several Apps beforehand that can help you when you're here. If you don't want to incur long-distance and data-roaming charges, put your phone on Airplane Mode then turn on your WiFi. You will be able to use your apps whenever you're in range of a logged-in WiFi.

WhatsApp is a useful phone, text, and video service that's free to use when both ends are connected to WiFi. Both ends must have WhatsApp installed on their phones for it to work. It's great for staying in touch with family back home because you can easily call one another for free anytime you want and for as long as you want. It also works when you're not on WiFi, but you will incur data charges for accessing the Internet. It is also widely used in Costa Rica. In fact, many businesses advertise their WhatsApp number on billboards.

Skype is the king of VoIP (Voice Over Internet Protocol) apps. It can work on both your phone and your computer. We've used it when we're talking over WiFi – computer to computer. Skype is free, but the person you're calling must also have it. Facebook Messenger is also a good tool.

Google Maps are indispensable for travel in Costa Rica. We recommend downloading the areas you are going to be visiting so

that you can access the maps without an Internet connection.

Waze, the traffic app is very popular in Costa Rica – more so than Google Maps. It also has the added advantage of giving you real-time updates on your route, such as a new traffic accident or police on the side of the road.

If you want to make local calls and use local cell service for Internet service, you must buy a SIM card after you arrive to replace the one in your phone (some Android phones have dual SIM card slots just for this purpose, so you have the best of both worlds, using each SIM card for different purposes).

For a different SIM card to work, your phone must be unlocked. If you're not sure, contact your U.S. carrier before you leave for Costa Rica. Your cell phone doesn't need to be "jailbroken" – that's something completely different.

WiFi service is available at many restaurants and coffee shops frequented by tourists; you just need to ask for the password. Since letters and spoken numbers are different in Spanish, it is often easier just to give the server your phone so they can enter your password. Once you have the password, it's possible to stand outside and pick up the signal. You'll sometimes see a group of young Ticos doing this on the sidewalk outside a coffee shop.

SIM Cards

You can buy a pay-as-you-go SIM card ("prepago" pre-PAH-go) for your smartphone when you land in Costa Rica. Rather than buy a card at the main airport in Alajuela, you can save money by taking a taxi to the nearby Walmart and getting it there.

Sim cards are cheap – about one mil – and you must show your passport to get one.

Once you buy the SIM card, you can take your phone off Airplane Mode. You'll then be connected to a Costa Rica carrier like Kolbi, Claro, or Movistar). You will pay for each minute you talk (but only when you make the call), every message you send, and each MB (megabyte) of internet use. You can reload it anywhere a sign for that carrier is displayed outside a business.

To add time to the SIM card, give the clerk your new phone number and pay whatever amount you want: one mil, two mil, three mil or more. You pay by price, not by minutes. You'll get a text message when your card is running low on minutes and it's time to add more. You should also get a text message when you pay to add minutes. You can recharge your sim card at any store displaying the logo of the card you are using out front. It's common to buy minutes while at the grocery check-out

20 HOTEL FORMALITIES

To really experience Costa Rica, you should avoid the big-name international chain hotels that don't give you a true sense of this magical country and its culture.

Costa Rica is full of boutique family-owned hotels, Bed and Breakfasts, and Eco-lodges. Our favorite resource for finding such gems is TripAdvisor.com, where we can read the most-recent reviews from fellow travelers and get tips for staying at a hotel.

Our only exception to not staying in chain hotels is our recommendation for the Courtyard Marriott near the main airport in Alajuela. This recommendation is based on the short distance from the hotel to the airport (walking distance, if you feel up to it) and its proximity to a Walmart, restaurants and walking distance the largest mall in Central America – City Mall. Courtyard Marriott has a free shuttle to and from the airport.

There is no other hotel in that airport/mall area.

Your Passport

You will be asked for your passport when you check in to a hotel, so be sure to have it handy. The hotel will usually make a copy of the front page of your passport and your entry stamp. Under no circumstances should you allow a hotel (or any other business) to keep your passport. Once someone has possession of your passport, you could face any number of problems trying to get it back. Not only is it your most valuable possession when traveling to a foreign country, but passports are a valuable commodity on the black market.

Every hotel is, by law, supposed to keep a guest list with a passport (or Costa Rican cedula) number. The police come around from time to time to make sure hotels are keeping up to date with that.

21 OTHER ACCOMMODATIONS

If you are traveling with an extended family, or with close friends, a vacation rental is a great option that will give you more privacy at a lower cost than a hotel.

There are thousands of rental houses available in Costa Rica with a variety of options, such as a daily maid service, a chef, private pool,.

We have friends who used this option for an extended family of about 30 people. The villa had six bedrooms, seven baths and four floors (11,000 square feet), overlooking the Pacific Ocean. They shopped locally and cooked almost every dinner at home, saving a lot of money. The villa provided daily maid service (three maids) who came in during the day while they were out and cleaned everything, including doing the dishes. It ran about $800 a night.

You can easily find two-bedroom houses or cabinas near the beach that go for much less than $100 a night during the "green season."

TripAdvisor.com is a good source for house rentals.

Airbnb

Airbnb rooms can be had for under $50 per night during the green season, all over Costa Rica. When booking a room, be sure to about the availability of WiFi, whether the property is on a paved road, and the availability of transportation such as buses. You do not want to get stuck in the middle of nowhere with a dirt road washing away during the rainy season and no access to local transportation.
Asking about local shops for groceries and restaurants can also be helpful for those who want to save money by cooking themselves. Even if you don't want to cook, most restaurants offer take out

service and it is common for them to have someone with a motorcycle who (for a small fee) will deliver your order straight to your door.

Hostels

Hostels abound in Costa Rica, as the country is a magnet for backpackers. Most popular tourist destinations have quite a number to choose from.

Don't limit your choices by thinking of hostels as shared bunk beds. Many hostels have private rooms with en-suite bathrooms available for a slightly higher price. Be sure and ask the same questions discussed above regarding the location.

Camping

If you really want to get out and become one with nature, perhaps you should consider camping. It's a great way to enjoy the country and save money. But, there's also a negative side: campgrounds without security are a target of thieves. One only has to read reviews of camping locations to read about theft, wandering drunks and dogs.

If you want to camp, consider only campgrounds with good reviews on TripAdvisor.

22 TOUR GUIDES

"Should we hire a tour guide?" The question always seems to come up.

If you are going to a national park, a tour guide is recommended because they know the park inside and out and can point out things, you'd probably miss without them. They also privately exchange information with other tour guides about where a particular animal can be spotted along the route.

Tour guides generally take a group of up to 10 people, so don't expect the person you hire will be your exclusive guide.

Double-check that they are ICT certified (*Instituto Costarricense de Turismo*). That means they have gone through the training, the courses and passed the test to be a certified guide. That includes a mastery of English or other languages. Many so-called "tour guides" aren't certified. The ones who are will wear the ICT identification card around their neck.

A good tour guide will have identification clearly displayed and carry a spotting scope and perhaps a book to show you photos or pictures of the animal he's talking about.

At many parks, "tour guides" can be found at the entrance, trying to solicit business. It's best to book through your hotel.

At Manuel Antonio, we didn't have a car and our tour guide picked us up at our hotel. He carried a spotting scope on a tripod and carried a wildlife book with photos of the animals he was pointing out. He would set up the scope, let his customers look through the scope at the animal and show us photos while talking about the animal's habits.

23 COSTA RICA FOOD

This is not Mexico. Most Costa Ricans don't like spicy food. There are, however, several pepper sauces available here for those who do. Our favorite is Chilero, a kind of smooth-tasting hot sauce.

You can also find some sodas and restaurants with Buffalo-style hot sauce for chicken wings. Be forewarned. It's pronounced "BOOF-ah-low" in Costa Rica. There are also knock-off versions of Tabasco.

Gallo Pinto

Gallo Pinto (GUY-oh PEEN-toh) is the national dish of Costa Rica. It consists of seasoned rice and beans.

Gallo Pinto translates as "spotted rooster." Gallo Pinto is traditionally a breakfast dish but can be eaten throughout the day or as a side dish.

Gallo Pinto is much more than rice and beans mixed together. The secret is the mirepoix or sofrito – a mixture of onion, carrot, celery and sweet pepper. Throw in some chopped cilantro at the end and splash on some Costa Rica Salsa Lizano and you've got yourself a meal. Top it with a fried egg for breakfast or mix in savory chunks of pork belly ("*chicharrones con carne*" chich-ah-ROAN-es con CAR neh) and you've got lunch.

Most tourist destination restaurants and those in bigger cities such as San José have menus in both English and Spanish but when venturing off to smaller towns such as those found in the Central Valley, this may not be the case. This is where those small pocket translation books can come in handy, but usually, there is a server who knows the English terms for the menu items.

If you are looking for smaller portion sizes, look for the *"Boca"* menu. These are considered appetizers but are often enough for a meal, especially lunch. Another option frequently available is a *medio* size or *grande* size. As with bocas, the medio size is usually plenty for a meal. Ordering bocas and medio sizes will save you money as well as give you an option to order two bocas to have two different meals for your lunch or dinner.

If you want to take your leftovers with you to eat later, point to your half-full dish and say *"Para llavar"* (PEAR-uh yuh-VAR)

At Your Table

Some Ticos eat French fries with a toothpick. Most Ticos also prefer both ketchup and mayonnaise on their fries. You should at least try it at least once that way. Condiments are offered two different ways depending on the restaurant. Some will bring you a small container with individual servings of the condiments. The container also has a small pair of scissors so you can open the serving packages without worrying about it squirting all over you. Other restaurants will offer bottles of the condiments. Keep in mind the yellow bottles are not mustard, they are mayonnaise. We have rarely seen mustard served as part of the condiments offered so do not be surprised if it is not available where you are eating. The same goes for black pepper (*"pimienta negra"* pee-MYEN-tah NEH-gruh). Here, it is usually as a pepper grinder.

Silverware is brought to the table once you have placed your order so the server will know what you need. For example, if you have ordered fish, you will not be needing a steak knife. Silverware is always covered in plastic to keep it clean.

24 RESTAURANTS VS SODAS

If you are driving somewhere and see a sign that says *"Soda"* it doesn't refer to soft-drinks. Sodas are different from restaurants (*Restaurantes*) because they are smaller and usually family-owned and operated. Here's a soda by the river that also rents cabins.

A Soda may have two to four or more tables for customers – almost always occupied by Ticos.

A Soda serves what is known as *"típico,"* or the typical Costa Rica meal. The basic plate is called a *"casado"* (cah-SAH-doh) which translates to "married." On the plate, you will find a "marriage" of meat, rice, beans, a plantain cooked in sugar (the long yellowish thing) and a fried egg.

Meats served in casados can be beef, pork (usually a pork chop), or fish. You get to choose the meat. All casados in a soda are the same, except for the meat portion. The casado sometimes includes a fruit drink.

You can never go wrong ordering a casado at a Soda if you are looking for the cheapest, most-filling meal for the smallest amount of money. There are other dishes offered as well, but usually at a little higher price. If you want to save money while in Costa Rica, eat at a Soda and order the casado.

Many Sodas don't have menus printed out but chalkboards or other handmade signage indicating what they have to offer, with the prices in colones. Sodas cater to Ticos and usually don't accept U.S. dollars. Sodas are typically only open for breakfast and lunch and do not offer alcohol as a beverage. You are free to bring own, however. (more about that later)

If the restaurant or soda has *"Mirador"* in the name, it usually has a good view.

Bocas

If you're looking for an appetizer-size portion of food, you'll find it in *bocas* (BOW-cas). Many restaurants have a separate Boca menu. If not, you can also ask the waiter for a boca-size of an entrée.

Bocas are especially good if you're just drinking beer or wine and want a little something to munch on.

Breakfast, Lunch & Dinner

This is how you say breakfast, lunch, and dinner in Spanish:

El Desayuno (el dee-say-OONO) - Breakfast

El Almuerzo (EL ahl-MWER-zoh) - Lunch

La Cena (lah SAY-nah) – Dinner

Food Preparation In Spanish

Here are the Spanish names for food and food preparation:

Beef is *carne* (CAR-neh). Pork is *cerdo* (SER-doh). Chicken is *pollo* (POY-yo) and fish is *pescado* (pes-CAH-doh).
Pollo a la plancha (POY-yo ah lah PLAHN-cha) = chicken, grilled
Pollo en salsa (POY-yo en SAL-suh) = chicken in sauce
Chuleta (chew-LET-ah) = a pork chop
Filet (fi-LET) = usually a fish filet. You can order this "*empanizado*" (breaded), "*al ajillo*" (in garlic and butter), "*a la plancha*" (grilled)
Carne en salsa (CAR-neh en SAL-suh) = beef in a gravy-like sauce
Arroz con camarón - (ah-ROSE con cam uh ROAN) = rice with shrimp (Our local Soda also has *camarón con arroz*, which has more (*mas*) shrimp, or larger shrimp, than the *arroz con camarón*)
Arroz con pollo (ah-ROSE con POY-yo) = rice with chicken
Bifstek (sounds like "beefsteak" said quickly as one word) = a small cut of beef. Costa Rica beef comes from Brahmas and is tough. Cuts of beef in Costa Rica don't conform to standard cuts in the United States.
Ensalada (en-suh-LAH-dah) - salad
Vino blanco (VEE-noh BLAHN-coh) White Wine
Vino Tinto (VEE-noh TEEN-toh) Red Wine
Beer is ordered by brand. There is no need to add the word "*cerveza*" to the brand name. Beer is also referred to as "*birra*" (BEER-rah).

Ice Water

There's no need to order bottled water in a restaurant or soda. The tap water is perfectly safe to drink here.

If you'd like a glass of ice water, ask for *"Vaso de agua con hielo, por favor."* *Hielo* (ice) is pronounced like "yellow" in English.

Water is not automatically served, and you will need to ask if you would like some. Often, a small pitcher of ice water is brought with the glass of water if multiple people are drinking it. This saves the server time and no need to interrupt your meal coming to ask if you want more water.

Where's The Check?

You should be aware that most Tico waiters will never bring your check before you ask for it. Ticos consider it rude to bring a check before it is requested. To them, it is the same thing as telling you to leave. Who knows? Maybe you wanted another cup of coffee or another drink? Many folks mistake this as slow service or laziness. Actually, the waiters are just being polite. Meals here are meant to be enjoyed in extended conversations, not rushed through. It's not uncommon to take 90 minutes to 2 hours at a table, especially if you're with friends. It's accepted. If they try to hurry you out, it's a tourist trap and they want to turn tables faster.

Unless you are at a fine dining type restaurant, your check will not be brought to your table unless you ask for it. Somewhere near the bar area you will see a booth (or sometimes just a cash register) with a sign that says *"Caja."* This is where you will pay for your meal. Simply go to the cashier and tell them what you had. Sometimes the servers will let the cashier know what you had. If you are splitting the bill, this is a great way to make sure you pay only for what you ate and drank rather than having a discussion among friends about who owes what. Everyone pays their fair share of taxes and tips.

The desire for servers at restaurants to make sure you have a quiet, uninterrupted meal can sometimes turn in to a bit of frustration until you get used to it. They will not hover around your table asking if you want something else or interrupt conversations asking if everything is okay. It is presumed if they are needed for something you will let them know. Don't get us wrong, they watch your table for a sign you need something. For example, if you would like another beer, just lift your empty (or almost empty) beer bottle for them to see and (depending on the server) they will usually just bring another beer or, in some cases, will check whether you want another beer or something different. For us, when we go to our regular restaurant, the servers know us and we just use hand gestures across the room to indicate whether we want another beer, another glass of wine, or one of each. Once you get used to it, it is nice not having your meal interrupted every five minutes by someone trying to turn your table for their next customer.

Tipping

There is usually a 10 percent tip included on your bill at most restaurants in Costa Rica and you are not obligated to tip additional unless you want. This tip is usually spread among the restaurant staff. Usually, one or two mil is enough.

DO NOT leave your change on the table as a tip. It is insulting as if you are saying "This is not enough for me to worry about so you can have it." When you leave an additional tip, hand it folded to your server personally with a friendly "*Para usted*" (PEAR-ah oo-STED), which means "For you."

25 PULPERIAS, GROCERY STORES & FERIAS

Small mom-and-pop groceries are called *pulperías* here. Think of them as neighborhood, family-owned and operated convenience stores. They usually have a few of each thing they sell. Since some Ticos don't have refrigerators or access to transportation, they visit the neighborhood pulperia every couple of days so they can buy just what's needed which can be carried home in a bag.

You can also pay your phone, water and electricity bills at many pulperias. Also, many sell propane in small tanks for kitchens or shower water heaters.

The name seems to have originated from when they sold fruit drinks, made from the pulp of the fruit. The name is sometimes shortened to *Pulpa*

Major Grocery Store Chains

Walmart (Mexico) is the king of the grocery store jungle in Costa Rica. Walmart not only has its signature brand store but Maxi Pali, Pali, Mas X Menos, and Perimercado.

On certain items, sometimes Walmart is cheaper than Maxi Pali or the other way around. Prices don't vary by much. You'll find larger selections of U.S. foods at Walmart.

Mas X Menos is like an upscale Walmart. The selection and prices reflect that.

The closest we've found to a no-membership U.S. grocery store is Auto Mercado. Again, better selection with more U.S. brands but higher prices.

PriceSmart is a members-only store with lots of American brands. The closest U.S. equivalent is Costco.

Some Things Aren't Refrigerated

When you visit a grocery store in Costa Rica you may be surprised to see some items unrefrigerated. The reason behind this is some Tico homes don't have refrigerators or have small refrigerators.

Items that are perfectly safe unrefrigerated here include eggs, milk, and some types of margarine. You can find refrigerated milk and margarine, too. The unrefrigerated milk is ultra-pasteurized and tastes the same as refrigerated milk. You will need to refrigerate it once it's opened, however. Eggs don't have to be refrigerated because the protective enzymes in the shells aren't washed away, as they are in some other countries. When you think about it, chickens don't lay eggs and then put them in a refrigerator to keep them from spoiling. Fertilized eggs are in the outside air until they hatch.

Ferias (Farmer's Markets)

Ferias are farmers markets that are open weekly in many towns in Costa Rica. They are the best place to buy the freshest produce and meats.

The ferias are usually open only Friday afternoons and Saturday mornings. Depending on the size of the town, they may be only open one day a week or as many as four days a week. Many people stock up for the week, lugging carts on wheels to haul their purchases home. You can also rent different sized grocery carts to push around the feria and put your fruits and veggies in.

We've found it's also good to bring along an insulated bag or cooler for cold meats, fish and cheese. A couple of small plastic bottles of pre-frozen water should be sufficient to keep the items in the bag cool until you get home. The best place to buy insulated bags is at Walmart or Maxi Palí (same company).

The first rule of the feria is don't buy from a vendor if the prices aren't clearly marked. If you do, you run the risk of "gringo pricing." That's a more expensive price quoted because you are a gringo. Elizabeth also noticed a price increase for the same product from the same vendor if she was her diamond wedding ring. So, always buy from vendors who have prices posted.

The price posted is usually per kilo, if it's meat, seafood or any heavy fruit or vegetable. This is not always the case but is usually the case.

When picking out fruits and vegetables, you indicate to the seller you want to buy something by picking one up from the pile. The vendor will usually grab a plastic bag and hold it open while you select the items and place them in the bag. When you're ready, you motion to him or say "listo" (LEE-stoh), which means "ready." He weighs it and gives you the price. If you don't understand Spanish, you can give him a mil (1,000 colones) and he will give you change.

Remember, you don't have to buy a full kilo of anything. You can buy one potato or one piece of fruit if you want. To order items smaller in weight than a kilo, you ask for the portion in grams. One kilo equals 1,000 grams (*gramos*). Since a kilo equals 2.2 U.S. pounds, a half-kilo ("*medio kilo*" MED-ee-oh KEY-low)is 1.1 U.S. pounds – about the closest you will get to a pound when ordering with the metric system. A half-pound would then be 500 grams (*gramos*). A quarter kilo would then be ("*dos cientos cincuenta gramos*") or 250 grams. When you get used to it, the metric system of weight is remarkably simple.

In the U.S. chicken breasts are usually sold per breast (one side). In Costa Rica, you'll find chicken breasts are two breasts connected. A chicken breast is called a *pechuga* (peh-CHOO-gah) in Costa Rica. It always means two breasts. If you indicate you want a pechuga, the vendor will pull one out and hold it up for you to see if it's the size you want. You can tell him "*perfecto*" or "*mas*" (more) or "*menos*" (smaller or less).

The same goes for the meat seller. For hamburger, called *Molida Especial* (moh-LEE-dah eh-speh-see-AHL), you can buy a kilo or any variation thereof. For example, a kilo is 2.2 pounds. If you want that separated into two bags you can ask for "*un kilo en dos bolsas*". He will then put 1.1 pound in each bag.

When buying any type of meat or poultry, the vendors use a plastic bowl for you to put your money in. You don't hand it directly to them because they have been handling meat or poultry. They'll extend the bowl. You place your money in the bowl, and they will carry the bowl to the cashier ("CAH-ha"). They'll return your change in the same bowl that you reach into to retrieve your change. If you have a large bill, such as a 10 or 20 mil, the meat guy is the best place in the Feria to use it and get change. They deal in larger amounts of money, as many people buy a week's worth of meat, and have more change.

Tangerines are called *mandarinas* in the Ferias. Limes are *limónes*. Yellow lemons are only found at specialty stores.

Central Markets

Mercado Centrals are located near the center of town. They are more permanent versions of ferias and are used for day-to-day shopping for Ticos who don't want their produce wrapped in plastic, on plastic trays.

Even if you're not shopping, it's fun to visit the Mercado Central. The biggest, most interesting one is in San Jose.

Beer

You can buy beer in most grocery stores in Costa Rica, which is convenient when you are stocking up on supplies for your hotel room or vacation house.

There are three national brands of beer in Costa Rica. The main one is *Imperial* (im-peer-ee-AL). It is a light lager with a 4.6 percent (by volume) alcohol content. We think it's equivalent to a Coors. It also comes in lower calorie versions: Imperial Light and Imperial Silver.

The second national brand is *Pilsen* (PEEL-sen), recognizable by its red and white label. Pilsen's alcohol content is 5.1 percent. It is also a light lager, but it has a more pronounced hops flavor. The beer been has been around in Costa Rica since 1888. It is equivalent to a Budweiser in the United States.

The third brand of local beer is *Bavaria*. It comes in Dark, Light, and Gold. The Dark is a Munich-Dunked-style German lager with a pronounced malt flavor. It contains 5 percent alcohol content.

All three are average. Costa Rica is not a haven for great-tasting, well-brewed beers. Microbreweries are just catching on and their bottled products are pricey. Luckily, imported beers are available.

Alcohol

The national alcoholic drink is *guaro* (distilled, fermented sugar came juice) and the national brand is *Cacique* (cah-SEE-kay). It is a sugar cane liquor of high purity and is the bestselling distilled spirit in Costa Rica. It is known as "Costa Rica liqueur" and it has a 30 percent alcohol content (60 proof).

Cacique has a neutral, slightly sweet taste and can be consumed straight (with a limon) or combined with any natural or artificial mixers. It is the equivalent to a white rum and should be taken chilled. *Miguelito* (me-gull-LEH-tow) is a drink made with coconut milk and *Cacique*.

It also comes in a more-refined black label (run through activated charcoal) and as *Ron Colorado* – regular Cacique with rum flavoring added, a kind of poor man's rum.

Cacique is a popular drink in Tico bars, drunk straight, mixed with soda or chased by a beer. If you like spicy alcoholic drinks, you might also order a *chiliguaro* which is Cacique mixed with some type of pepper or hot sauce and other flavorings.

Wine is not commonly consumed in Costa Rica (especially white) and it is not unusual to find a restaurant which serves beer and other alcohol but not wine. If the price of wine is not listed on the menu, be sure and ask before ordering. We once got "gringo'd" at a restaurant where the wine price was not listed and when the bill came, we discovered one glass of wine was seven mil (approximately $12). It was the last time we made that mistake.

If you go to a restaurant or soda where alcohol is not served, it is perfectly acceptable to bring in your own. We have some friends who commonly bring a cooler with wine and beer to restaurants where alcohol is not served. The restaurant will provide a glass and (if needed) ice for your drinks.

26 BANKS & ATMS

Banks in Costa Rica fall into two categories: national banks and private banks.

The National banks include *Banco Nacional de Costa Rica* (shortened to Banco Nacional), *Banco de Costa Rica,* and *Bancrédito*.

Private banks include BAC San José, Banco Popular, and Banco Davivienda.

If you're a gringo, we've found the private banks are generally the most receptive. They also offer faster service, shorter lines, and more English-speaking staff.

Don't be alarmed if you see a security guard wearing a bullet-proof vest and sporting a large handgun. Some stand outside the bank. Most stand inside.

Banking is a serious business and you should dress appropriately. No flip flops, shorts or muscle shirts. Your attire and demeanor will be noticed by the teller and can result in a friendly transaction or one where they make it as hard as possible for you.

When entering a bank, you should remove your hat and/or sunglasses. You'll likely be reminded by a guard if you forget. In larger banks, such as state banks, you'll be directed to a number machine to retrieve your number. The instructions are in Spanish so you may need to ask for help. The ticket will have a letter and a number on it. Watch for your ticket and number on electronic screens above the tellers. The numbers are also announced over a loudspeaker in Spanish.

Seating arrangements in large banks that don't use numbered tickets sometimes include a single line of chairs from front to back next to the normal seating section. These chairs are reserved for elderly and handicapped customers. If you fall into either category you should take the empty chair nearest the teller windows. As the front chairperson is called to the teller window, the person who had been seated behind them moves up to the vacant seat. As in most situations in Costa Rica, it is customary for men to allow women to go ahead of them.

You should have your passport with you when conducting any bank transaction. Sometimes they ask for it and sometimes they don't. It's best to have it just in case.

Automatic Teller Machines

Don't use an ATM that not connected to a bank if you can avoid it. The reason is if the machine eats your card you know where to go to retrieve it. Also, keep in mind it can take three days (or more) before your card will be returned.

Many ATMs in Costa Rica have English options, which make it easier for you to deal with the various screens. Getting colones from ATM'S takes a bit of getting used to because there's no comma and the decimal is in a different place than U.S. ATMs. Three-hundred thousand colones, which is 300,000 colones or 300 mil, comes out on the ATM readout as 300000.00 (with no comma).

Something you must do when entering a bank or attached ATM is remove your hat and/or sunglasses. It's not a courtesy, it's so the ATM camera can get a good photo of you. If you don't, you run the risk of being prodded by the bank security guard who watches the front door or the bank and the ATM.

Personally, we wouldn't use an ATM if there is not a guard keeping an eye on things. (**Never use an ATM at night**)

Be sure to quickly remove your card from the machine after taking your money. If you don't, the machine may keep it. This is done as a safety step in case the customer walks away from the ATM, leaving their card.

David had the experience of forgetting to take his credit card out of an ATM and walked away. Discovering he had forgotten his card a short while later, he rushed back to the ATM to find his card gone. Inquiring inside at the bank he was told the card couldn't be retrieved for 72 hours for security reasons. He returned each day to inquire about the card and the bank employee he had been dealing with finally gave it to him 48 hours after it had been taken by the machine. He had to provide his passport to prove his identity. So, avoid that hassle and make sure to take your card out of the machine promptly.

The national Costa Rica banks have come up with a way to get more money out of the transaction: some began limiting withdrawals to $200 USD. That way, you must make two withdrawals to get to $300 and the banks collect two transaction fees.

We've found that the BAC San José (ATMs and branches at many major tourist areas) charges the lowest fee for withdrawals ($3 vs $5) and also has the highest limit for withdrawals (currently around $500).

27 SHOPPING

In Costa Rica, as in the rest of Latin America, most small shops (la tiendas – lah-tee-EN-dahs) are privately owned. When you enter a small shop or store, you are entering the owner's property – just like walking into their home. In Costa Rica, is customary to exchange pleasantries, even if you don't know the owner, as you would if you were visiting their home.

'Gringo Pricing'

Yes, there is a thing called "Gringo Pricing" in Costa Rica. It's when you get charged more than the Tico price.

The best way to avoid Gringo pricing is to shop where prices are clearly marked or displayed – even in the *feria* (Farmer's Market). Make it a point not to buy where prices aren't shown.

Gringo pricing also happens when a gringo walks into a shop or store and begins immediately saying, "I want that and that and that. How much?" That's not polite and you may pay for your mistake.

The proper way to shop is to say hello (*Hola!*) to the clerk and ask how they are doing (*¿Cómo estás?* KO-mo eh-STAHS). They will most likely say "*Bien*" and ask how you are doing (*¿Bien y tú?* beYEN ee TWO). You answer "*Bien*" or "*Pura Vida!*" (poo-rah vee-dah!)

After that, you can start looking around or asking for something.

A few pleasantries and an honest interest in the welfare of the person you are dealing with will go a long way in endearing them to you, so you don't get gringo pricing.

Souvenir Shopping

Don't buy souvenirs at the airport. They are marked up considerably in the last-minute gift shops. Remember they must pay their overhead for doing business there.

Instead, buy souvenirs at the grocery store or other stores in the town you are visiting.

The same advice goes for coffee, chocolate, and such. You'll find local coffee brands and better prices at the grocery store.

Always ask if there's a discount for paying cash.

28 PHARMACIES

Gringos sometimes mispronounce the word *"farmacia."* It is not farm-uh-SEE-uh but rather far-MAS-ee-ah.

Most pharmacies in Costa Rica have a pharmacist who is on site and will give you free consultations for minor ailments. Many will also take your blood pressure for free.

Farmacias are a great place to go if you aren't feeling well but not bad enough to make an appointment with a regular doctor. You walk in, ask if they speak English (*"¿Habla inglés?"* AH-bah een-GLESS) and then describe your symptoms. Just in case, you should translate your symptoms from English with the Google Translate app or something similar. That way, you can just hand them your phone with a list of your symptoms.

You can also hand them your U.S. medicine, or give them the name on a piece of paper and they will look up the equivalent available in Costa Rica.

Many pharmaceuticals that require a prescription in the United States are over the counter in Costa Rica. Otherwise, the pharmacist who is on-staff will probably write you a prescription. Medicines in Costa Rica usually come from North, Central, or South America.

Be sure to mention if you're paying cash (in colones) so you can get the cash discount. The word for cash is *"efectivo"* (e-feck-TEEVO) or *"dinero efectivo* (di-NER-oh e-feck-TEEVO). Most ask if you're paying *efectivo* or *credito* before ringing up the purchase. They print out the receipt for you, keeping a copy with the medicine. You are then directed to a special window (*"caja"* KAH-hah) where you pass the receipt and money to the cashier. "They then give you your medicine in a stapled, white plastic bag.

121

You'll find the farmacias with the largest selection somewhere across the street from the central park in any community. The central park is always located in front of the main church in town. Larger places such as San Jose will have several parks, but for most towns there is only one.

Macrobioticas

Macrobioticas are the Costa Rica version of health food stores. You can find a full range of health food and supplements in them, but some even have Asian food products.

A local macrobiotica in our town carries a full range of Asian food and sauces – things that we can't find in our local grocery store. Our macrobiotica also carries Himalayan rock salt, if that's something you can't live without

Even if you're not into health food, macrobioticas are worth checking out to see what's available.

29 INSECTS & SNAKES

There are about 34,000 species of insects in Costa Rica, so be forewarned. The most common species is the ant ("Hormiga" or- MEE-gah). You'll also find lots of spiders and scorpions.

One type of ant is called a Bullet Ant. It is said that its sting is the worst of any insect on earth. A sting from a bullet ant can cause local paralysis and pain for up to 24 hours. One insect expert described the pain as "Pure, intense, brilliant pain. like walking over flaming charcoal with a 3-inch nail embedded in your heel."

Next to that, a scorpion sting is relatively minor. Contrary to what you'd think, the sting of the smaller scorpion is said to be more painful than stings from larger scorpions. David has only been stung by a large scorpion, so he can't give you an accurate comparison. Remember, shake out your shoes every morning before putting your feet in them. Better yet, wear flip-flops! (Scorpion in Spanish is "escorpion"YON) .

If you are stung, the pain should last for 15 to 20 minutes. There are no deadly poisonous scorpions in Costa Rica, according to experts.

Costa Rica has lots of spiders, but they eat lots of insects. The largest spider species in Costa Rica is the tarantula, such as the Costa Rican Tiger Rump, Costa Rican Bluefront Tarantula, or the Costa Rican Zebra Tarantula.

The Orb Weaver Spider (pictured), with large spindly legs, is very common in Costa Rica. They build spiral wheel-shaped webs that are often found in gardens, fields and low forests.

Small insects such as flies, moths, beetles, wasps, and mosquitoes are examples of insects that make up the spider's diet. Some larger orb weavers may also trap and eat small frogs and hummingbirds should they venture into the web.

Orb weavers rarely bite and only do so when threatened and unable to escape. If bitten by an orb weaver, the bite and injected venom is comparable to that of a bee sting, with no long-term implications unless the bite victim happens to be hyper-allergic to the venom.

Snakes

There are more than 150 species of snakes in Costa Rica and 22 species are poisonous. Anti-venom is not readily available of the Central Valley.

The fer-de-lance pit viper (Latin: Bothrops asper), also known as the "terciopelo" by Ticos, is one of the world's most venomous. It is also the most aggressive in Costa Rica, racking up the most recorded bites on humans – between 70 and 100 a year. It can reach lengths of up to 10 feet. It is recognizable by its triangular-shaped head and a black "X" pattern on its back.

Its name is derived from a French expression, meaning "iron of the lance" or "spearhead".

The fer-de-lance inhabits the humid lowlands and can frequently be found coiled among the leaf litter on the jungle floor.

Other poisonous snakes in Costa Rica include the Bushmaster. Its genus Latin name (Lachesis) comes from a Greek word that refers to one of the "Three Fates" in Greek mythology that determined the length of mortal lives.

Bushmaster snakes are nocturnal, and human bites are quite rare. However, the Bushmaster is capable of multiple bite strikes and the injection of large amounts of venom. Even the bite of a juvenile specimen can be fatal. However, this snake is rarely encountered, so snakebite incidents are not common. It has venom is so powerful that a bite from even a juvenile can be fatal. The snake can grow to 15 feet, making it the longest venomous snake in the Western Hemisphere.

The Eyelash Pit Viper is another poisonous snake you may see in Costa Rica. This species is characterized by a wide array of color variations, as well as the protruding scales above the eyes, giving it the appearance of having eyelashes. They can be most likely found coiled in trees.

Costa Rica also has Coral snakes, which are poisonous.

Printed in Great Britain
by Amazon